Jesus of Nazareth

Jesus of Nazareth

Dorothee Soelle and Luise Schottroff

Translated by John Bowden

For Ben
in friendship
Luise

Westminster John Knox Press
LOUISVILLE • LONDON

First published in May 2000 by Deutscher Taschenbuch Verlag, Munich

Copyright © 2000 Deutscher Taschenbuch Verlag GmbH & Co, KG, Munich

Published in Great Britain in 2002 by
Society for Promoting Christian Knowledge
Holy Trinity Church
Marylebone Road
London NW1 4DU

First published in the United States in 2002 by
Westminster John Knox Press
Louisville, KY 40202–1396

Translation copyright © 2002 John Bowden

Designed by Martin Sulzer-Reichel

British Library Cataloguing-in-Publication Data
A catalogue record for this book is available from the British Library

ISBN 0–281–05457–6

Library of Congress Cataloging-in-Publication Data is on file
at the Library of Congress, Washington, D.C.

ISBN 0–664–22500–4

Printed in Singapore

Contents

1. Reliquary for a thorn from Jesus' crown of thorns. Goldsmith's work, 1347–49. Baltimore, The Walters Art Museum.

Introduction

The most important sources for Jesus of Nazareth are the New Testament Gospels. The people whose voices can be heard in the Gospels spoke of Jesus because he gave them power—although he was already dead. They were not historians writing history, but spoke of him in the language of faith. So it is impossible to write a biography of Jesus in the precise sense of the word. Nevertheless the portrait in the Gospels, painted by faith, gives us a picture from which we can read historical information, above all if Jesus and his friends are understood even after his death as members of a largely homogeneous movement within Judaism. It was only with the fundamental change in the social structure of the Jesus movement after the middle of the second century AD, when it became a hierarchically ordered institution, that the picture of

2. View of the Mount of Olives and the Garden of Gethsemane.

Jesus also changed and took on dogmatic and hierarchical features. The separation of 'Christianity' from Judaism accompanies this change. So in the first century the word 'Christianity' has to be used on the understanding that the Christianity of this time is not yet a central institution, but a free association of communities which developed a lifestyle that fascinated many people. Christians understood themselves as part of Judaism and were filled with the conviction that Jesus of Nazareth was the Messiah long desired by the Jewish people.

In terms of method, there are three new features in this book about Jesus written by two women theologians:

- its feminist approach, which takes seriously the role, the function and the influence of women and verifies the original Christian approach that 'there is neither male nor female but all are one in Christ' (Gal. 3.28) historically in the story of Jesus;
- its liberation-theological approach, which begins from the 'last' (Matt. 20.16) in society and takes seriously their capacity to go on writing the Bible, because it spells out again the priority of the praxis of Christian life over doctrine, orthodoxy;
- the way in which it grapples with the centuries of Christian anti-Judaism and listens to the voices of Jewish conversation partners after the Shoah. They lead to self-critical work on the Christian tradition which seeks to end the hostility of the daughter religion towards the mother religion.

In order to make clear the indissoluble connection between Jesus and those who have been touched and inspired by him, we have set poetical Jesus texts from the present day alongside the historical accounts.

1

The Power of Legends: Birth and Childhood

The Gospel of Luke begins with a story of two ordinary Jewish women called Elizabeth and Mary. An extraordinary experience, a miracle, happens to both of them. Both are childless, both become pregnant. Elizabeth, who is very old and has never had a child in her long life (Luke 1.7), so that many people regard her as useless, conceives John. Mary, a very young girl ('virgin', Luke 1.27) of perhaps thirteen or fourteen, becomes the mother of Jesus.

3. Depiction of a woman in the Villa of the Mysteries in Pompeii, *c.* 60 BC.

In ancient society **virgin** was a term used to denote young girls of marriageable age who were to be given by their fathers in marriage. Only in later centuries is the word 'virgin' interpreted in terms of sexual intactness, which in dogmatic thought about Mary was thought to continue even after pregnancy and birth. Both the miraculous 'virgin birth' of Jesus and the negative evaluation of feminine sexuality bound up with it are ideas which occur in some Christian texts only around 100 and 150 years after the New Testament Gospels; they later became the starting point for the dogmas about Mary. One particularly pernicious development was that in later Christianity the idea of Eve's daughters as seducable seducers came to be associated with the cult of Mary. This led to an opposition between the pure virgin Mary and women as Eve's daughters, whose sexuality was depicted as unclean and sinful.

Both women, one at the beginning of her adolescence, the other at the end of her life, have had an experience of God which makes them new people, prophetesses. Their joy is expressed in experiences which only women can have: the child in Elizabeth's body, later to be John, greets the child in Mary's body by kicking. Then in the words of the tradition (I Sam. 2.1–10) Mary sings the Magnificat, the song of justice for the whole earth, one of the great Christian texts.

It was Elizabeth's wonderful experience that she became pregnant despite her age. An angel predicted that her son would become God's forerunner, who would free his people. Zechariah, the child's father, sings a hymn of praise to God: 'And you, child, shall be called a prophet of the Most High, for you shall go before God to prepare his way and to give knowledge of salvation to the people' (Luke 1.68–79). Here already it is evident that the people in whose midst this legend is set are in distress, that they long for liberation from political injustice. Their longing does not remain inactive. They tell of women prophets and forerunners of the God of liberation. The legends surrounding the birth of Jesus are a means of strengthening people who 'sit in darkness' so that they become capable of getting out of the darkness.

Mary similarly becomes pregnant in a miraculous way. She is betrothed to Joseph. An angel announces her pregnancy and proclaims with solemn words from the Bible that her son will be the Messiah of Israel. Messiah means a king sent from God, who unlike the kings of the earth will bring about righteousness and overcome the threat to the people (Luke 1.31–33). Mary reacts in a matter-of-fact way: how could I become pregnant without sexual intercourse (Luke 1.34)? The angel replies: the divine power will create the child in you, as wonderfully as the child which the old woman Elizabeth is bearing in her body.

Legends (the Middle Latin term for something 'to be read') are stories which invite emulation and imitation. A historical perspective which regards them as irrelevant is inadequate, as is a dogmatic perspective which turns them into doctrinal statements the acceptance of which decide whether one is a Christian or not. Both perspectives miss the point and tend towards a throw-away mentality which tolerates neither heretical doubt nor anything that cannot be proved factually.

The role of the mother of Jesus cannot be understood without the Jewish tradition. No dogma is being established here, nor is the intact virgin declared 'clean'. In Jewish thought God is regarded as the giver of life who opens the womb or leaves it closed, as is shown by many stories about women in the Hebrew Bible. God, not Jacob or another man, is the creator of life, and what Sarah, Rebecca and Rachel have experienced also applies to Mary: a pregnancy which is experienced as a miracle, as an act of God, and not as the consequence of sexual intercourse.

The different legends speak of pregnancy and birth as mysterious events and in so doing take up the tradition. They see these events as the treasure which gives people hope and raises them up. 'God has ended the humiliation of his slave,' sings Mary in her song of jubilation, and thus puts herself in the ranks of the matriarchs. In the Greek Bible of the Jews, the Septuagint, the word *tapeinosis* used here often denotes experiences of violence, including rape, and that particular humiliation of women is emphasized here.

The text tells of the miracle of a pregnancy without

Mary
The night when she first gave
  birth had been
cold. But in later years
she completely forgot
the frost in the beams above her
  pain and smoking ovens
and the strangling of the choking
  towards morning.
But above all she forgot the
  bitter shame
of not being alone,
which is the fate of the poor.
Mainly because of that
in later years it became the feast
  at which
everything was present.
The rough chatter of the
  shepherds fell silent.
Later in the story they became
  kings.
The wind, which was very cold,
became the angels' song.
Indeed, of the hole in the roof,
  which let in the frost,
there remained only
the star which looked in.
All this
came from the face of her son,
  who was gentle,
loved song,
invited the poor to him.
And had the custom
of living among kings,
and seeing a star above him at
  night time.
                    Bertolt Brecht

the involvement of a male; but at the same time it paints the picture of a girl who becomes pregnant outside marriage, whose humiliation is ended by the divine miracle and who becomes the prophetess of righteousness.

Mary's prophetic song is the climax of these legends: 'My soul magnifies the Eternal One, and my spirit rejoices in God, my help; for God has ended the humiliation of his slave' (Luke 1.46-55).

In praise of God, she sings how God has 'cast down the mighty from their thrones and exalted the humiliated': this is God's revolution. The poor are filled and the rich have to earn their own living, for their hands are now empty. The powerful rulers of the world-wide Roman empire lose their power, for they have arrogantly abused it. The young girl Mary is humiliated and the impoverished Jewish people become God's beloved children. All the promises of the history of Israel have been fulfilled. The song presupposes a precise critical analysis of the economic and political situation of the Jewish people, subjugated by Rome. Modern social history reckons that at this time there was a social split between rich and poor, and that 99% of the population could be called poor. The Magnificat uses the language of the religious tradition, that of the Psalms, to spell out the social situation. Measured by the reality of the people who sang this song, its dimensions of hope have a touch of megalomania. The intention is to contrast the reality of their actual existence and the justice that they hope for. For the contrast is also repeated at the narrative level, in the legend. The prophetic singer Mary is a poor child from Galilee. The rulers in Rome would not have found on any of their maps the Jewish villages in which the legends

Meditation on Luke 1
My soul sees the land of freedom
and my spirit will emerge from
   intimidation
the empty faces of the women will
   be filled with life
and they will become those
expected by generations before us
who were sacrificed.

God has done great things in me
he casts down the mighty from
   their thrones
and raises up those who have
   been trampled on.
Mercy will appear
when the dependent give up their
   wasted life
and learn to live for themselves.
         Dorothee Soelle

of the birth of Jesus are located. The claim of the song is heightened by the use here of the future rather than the past. Not only does God promise a just future: the claim is that it has already begun.

This gospel of the poor has often been painful or threatening for later Christian interpreters: turning things completely upside down may perhaps have been the hope of those with nothing, who picture themselves leading a life of luxury in the villas of the rich. There have been individual interpreters who have called this hope for a reversal of circumstances 'sub-Christian' and have wanted to remove it from the real 'authentic' tradition about Jesus as supposedly being a relic of his Jewish environment. However, most Western interpreters have reinterpreted the gospel of the poor and made it usable for middle-class Christianity. They have said—and this is still the predominant teaching in Western exegesis—that both

4. Rebecca and Eliezer. An illustration from the sixth-century 'Vienna Genesis'. Most Romans were completely ignorant of places in Israel and life there.

Mary's song and the message of Jesus criticize only unjust riches. Those who deal responsibly with their possessions are not put in question by Jesus.

Mary's song anticipates the heart of Jesus' message—or repeats it, if we take into account the late date at which these legends came into being. The people who are speaking here know that Jesus was executed. In Mary's song, Jesus' life is interpreted as the beginning of world-wide justice. That is also the way in which Jesus interpreted and shaped his career.

The powerful legends about the birth of Jesus hardly satisfy today's needs for historical facts. Luke 2.1–20, the 'Christmas story', tells how it came about that Jesus' parents—Mary was by then in an advanced state of pregnancy—had to travel from the insignificant village of Nazareth in Galilee to Bethlehem, the city of David. A Roman census required this, because Joseph's family traced its origins back to David. Thus Jesus was born not in Nazareth but in Bethlehem, in the city of David, from which the Jewish people expected the Messiah. This account of his birth in Bethlehem will likewise be a legend. The aim of the legend is also to show by his place of birth that Jesus is Messiah. In fact he was probably born in Nazareth.

The 'Christmas story' tells of the birth of the Messiah and in content is a continuation of Mary's song. There in Rome sits an emperor who can order a comprehensive census. Here in Bethlehem a child is born—in a stable of nomadic shepherds. The emperor in Rome speaks of world-wide peace, the *Pax Romana*. What is supposed to be world-wide peace, the *Pax Romana*, does not hide its ugly face, its poverty and violence, even in remote villages. But the whole of God's court reveres this child: 'Peace on earth' (Luke 2.1). The illegitimate

There is also contradictory information in the sources about the **year of Jesus' birth**. According to Luke 2.1 it falls in the reign of Augustus (37 BC – AD 14). The Gospels of Matthew and Luke say that Jesus was born during the lifetime of Herod the Great (i. e. 4 BC at the latest) (Matt. 2.1ff.; Luke 1.5).

But Quirinius, who according to Luke 2.1 had a census carried out, was the Roman governor of Syria only from AD 6. In fact he held a census in AD 6/7, but this was only a local one (Luke 2.1 differs). So it is impossible to establish the precise date of Jesus' birth.

child of a poor mother becomes the centre of the world. Here begins the peace that is to embrace the whole earth.

The Christmas story is a legend which presumably came into being only after Jesus' death. It speaks of the hopes of many people which took shape in Jesus' life and did not cease after his death.

We know little about Jesus' childhood years. Legends describe the life of the son of Jewish parents who, in faithful observance of the law, is circumcised on the eighth

5. The birth: a picture from Venezuela.

day after his birth (Luke 2.21) and already as a child learns to read the Torah and to discuss its interpretation with a knowledge of the text. The story of the twelve-year-old Jesus (Luke 2.41–52) shows him an attentive student of the Torah, who even after the Passover feast which the family celebrate together in the temple remains behind in order to discuss with the scribes in accordance with Jewish custom. His parents seek him in vain for three days, and when they rebuke him, he replies, 'Do you not know that I must be about my Father's business' (Luke 2.49). Here, in Jesus' separation from his parents before puberty, is a sign which is

In this night
the stars left their appointed
    places
and kindled wildfire tidings
in a sonic boom.

In this night
the shepherds left their posts
to shout new words
into one another's clogged ears.

In this night
the foxes left their warm caves
and the lion shook his head
'this is the end,
revolution'.

In this night
roses fooled the earth
and began to blossom
in the snow.

Dorothee Soelle

6. The birth of
Jesus. Fresco in
the Peribleptos
Church, Mistra,
Greece, late
fourteenth
century.

formulated more sharply and unconditionally later, when
Jesus has already begun to teach and heal.

When his mother and his brothers want to speak with him
but cannot get to him because of the crowd of people, a message is brought to him: 'Look, your mother and your brothers
are outside asking for you.' His answer sounds curt: 'Who are
my mother and my brothers?' And looking around at those
who are sitting around him, he says, 'Here are my mother
and my brothers! Whoever does the will of God is my brother,
and sister, and mother' (Mark 3.33–35). The fellowship of his
successors is not formed by family relationships—or by ethnic

Herod the Great (73/72–4 BC)
was appointed *strategos* (governor)
of Galilee by his father Antipater.
In 40 he fled to Rome, where in
39 the senate proclaimed him king
of Judaea. He conquered his realm
with the help of Roman mercenaries. From then on he ruled
Palestine like a modern state of a
Hellenistic Roman kind and was
able to keep the Romans at a
distance with rich gifts of money.
A politician and diplomat with a
shrewd financial sense, he erected
a new temple in Jerusalem and
developed the port of Caesarea,
but reacted to threats, supposed or
real, with brutal harshness.

and cultural relationships either—but by lifestyle, which here is designated by the simple words 'do the will of God'.

The most important legend from Jesus' early childhood is that of the murder of the children in Bethlehem. It reports how the brutality of the political ruler of the land intervenes in Jesus' early life, even before he is two years old. Matthew 2.13–18 tells how Herod the Great wanted to have Jesus killed as soon as he heard that the Messiah had been born in Bethlehem. As he could not discover which child in Bethlehem was meant, he had all the children aged two years old and younger in Bethlehem and the surrounding region put to death. Warned by the prophecy of an angel, Jesus' parents fled to Egypt in time. Biblical critics think that the legend of the murder of the children is completely unhistorical, as it cannot be verified by extra-biblical sources about Herod the Great. Yet this made-up story contains the whole truth of what the Jewish people suffered under Herod the Great. Herod used murder as a political weapon; he tortured the people and enriched himself and his family at the cost of men

7. The massacre of the innocents in Bethlehem. Pictures on a winged altar, Bavaria, end of the fifteenth century. Diocesan Museum, Freising. For a long time paintings in churches also served as 'visual aids' in the teaching of illiterate people; as a result the 'lessons' could be very vivid.

and women's lives. The legend of the murder of the children catches the outrage of his subjects and their spirit of resistance. A refugee child embodies God's mercy on the suffering Jewish people.

On 28 December, which in Catholicism is celebrated as the Feast of the Massacre of the Innocents, the North American peace movement often holds a celebration of its own. Friends of peace go to the Pentagon in Washington DC and shed human blood—their own—on the white desks of the officials who work on armaments there. In this way they connect the arms race and the deadly impoverishment of peoples with the Jesus tradition and dramatize the relationship between the *Pax Romana* and the *Pax Americana* by recalling Herod's murder of the children.

The composition of the Gospels
The Gospel of Luke belongs with the Acts of the Apostles as a single literary work. The text as a whole must have been composed between AD 70 and AD 90. The Gospel of Luke presupposes the Gospel of Mark and probably also other sources which already existed in writing (the so-called Logia source Q and the special material—texts which can be found only here and not in the other Gospels). All the Gospels went through a long process of origination, both oral and written. Many women and men took part in this process, so it makes sense in these texts to listen to the voices of many people for whom Jesus meant so much that they kept wanting to go on telling stories about him. In the early church each of the Gospels was attributed to a particular authority, in the case of Luke's Gospel to Luke the physician. In the New Testament he is mentioned in Col. 4.14, etc. These attributions of the Gospels are misleading since they suggest the notion of an individual—male—author and force into the background the many women and men whose voices can be heard in the texts.

2

The Beginning: Baptism and Temptation

Flavius Josephus writes about a messianic prophet in the first century: 'Around this time someone came from Egypt to Jerusalem who said that he was a prophet. He led the people astray, causing them to go with him to the so-called Mount of Olives, which lies over against the city and is about five stadia (just over half a mile) from it. He said that he wanted to show them from there how at his command the walls of Jerusalem would fall down. In this way, he promised, he would make it possible for them to enter the city. When Felix (the Roman governor) learned of this, he had soldiers take up arms, and with numerous cavalry and foot soldiers he set out from Jerusalem and attacked the followers of the Egyptian. He killed four hundred of them and took two hundred of them captive. However, the Egyptian himself escaped the battle and disappeared' (Josephus, *Antiquities* 20).

8. Flavius Josephus.
   Posterity is far better informed about Jewish history in the first century AD than about other historical periods. The Jewish historian **Josephus** (died shortly after AD 100) left behind extensive—and highly readable—descriptions of the history of Judaism in his time. He was a Jewish scholar with an extraordinarily good education and took part in the Jewish War against the Romans in AD 66–70 as commander of Galilee. When he was taken prisoner by the Roman army he prophesied to the Roman general Vespasian that Vespasian would become emperor. As a result he was welcomed into leading Roman circles and watched the rest of the War through Roman eyes. Later, he lived in Rome. His works are written from the perspective of the Roman leaders and are very critical of Jewish rebels against Rome.

There is life before death
Jesus, the great man of sorrows
on the cross, in the splendour of
    his wounds
he had his vision in death
and all the world saw his distress
and when the people three days
    afterwards
discovered his empty tomb
and found no body
they were glad. For they knew:
the man has risen
—there is a life after death!

Execution! There! Look at the
    communard
standing before the rifles
as Picasso painted him
trousers down, against the wall
the fat red fellow stands there
and cries and laughs at the same
    time
see him turn his arse towards
    death!
I have it, painted red on white
the painter's picture proves it
—there is a life after death.

The little Biermann thinks to
    himself:
Yes, yes: I think that's right
there is resurrection! Because
I myself am an example of it:
My dead father is alive? Even
the fools, the Don Quixotes!
In the freedom fight of humankind
there are no dead dead.
That is as true as dry bread:
—there is a life after death.

Note
Oh, if only afterwards there is
still something beautiful,
comforting in our situation.
How good! And yet, we are still
    left with
the little—the big—the question
(we would very much like to
    know that as well!)
Whether there is also
    something—we would love to
    know
—like a life before our death.
                    Wolf Biermann

This messianic prophet, whose name is unknown ('the Egyptian', i. e., a Jew born in Egypt), gathered people around him who hoped that God would now establish his kingdom on earth in favour of the Jewish people. The Hebrew Bible (Josh. 6) tells us that God made the walls of the strongly fortified city of Jerusalem fall down when the Jewish people circled it. The sound of the trumpets was enough to make the walls collapse. The Egyptian takes up this old story: Remember, God helped us then and he will help us now. Just as the walls of Jericho fell, so too the walls of Jerusalem, behind which the Roman military have esconced themselves, will fall now. We will enter Jerusalem and drive out the Romans. God is coming to our help, now! Then true peace will prevail on earth—for ever.

Like Felix in this case, the Roman governors thought that messianic movements such as these were politically dangerous and proceeded against the unarmed people with military force.

There were many messianic prophets like 'the Egyptian' among the Jewish people—and frequent attacks by the Roman army on these groups. They were inspired by hope for God's kingdom in heaven and on earth. They trusted in a God who in the course of Jewish history intervened time and again in favour of the little people. Rome understood the mood of this religion quite correctly when it reacted with military force. But the Roman leaders did not understand that the power of memory and hope for God filled the whole people and not just a few lunatics. When 'the Egyptian' and his followers were killed, others arose—in the name of the God of Israel.

Mark 1.14 f. says: 'Now after John ('the Baptist') was arrested, Jesus came into Galilee, preaching the gospel of God, and saying, "The time is fulfilled, and the kingdom of God is at hand; repent, and believe in the gospel.' John the Baptist—like 'the Egyptian' and also like Jesus of Nazareth—was one of the Jewish messianic prophets. In the wilderness he proclaimed the coming of God. He had publicly criticized Herod Antipas, who like his father Herod the Great was vassal king by the grace of Rome, for marrying his own sister-in-law

9. John the Baptist in the wilderness. Painting by Raphael, c. 1516. Paris, Musée du Louvre.

(Mark 6.17). John was politically inconvenient for Rome and Herod Antipas; he was arrested and later executed. When John had been silenced by his arrest, Jesus of Nazareth made a public appearance and proclaimed the coming of the kingdom of God. In this brief sentence, which links the arrest of John the Baptist and the first public appearance of Jesus, the structure of the anti-Roman resistance in the Jewish people becomes evident. From the perspective of a present-day critical history, Jesus was a messianic prophet in the Jewish people like many before him, in his time and after him. All the legends which have been told of him and all the facts which can be said to be historically reliable belong in this framework of the Jewish messianic hope and the liberation movements in the first century of our era.

Jesus had himself baptized by John the Baptist (Mark 1.9–11). For him, as for the many people who wanted baptism, this rite sealed the conversion of the person being immersed in the water to God and the assurance of God's nearness. Thus in his career Jesus moved from being a follower of John the Baptist to acting in public as a messianic prophet.

Whether Jesus thought that he was the Messiah is hard to establish, but historically it is quite possible. At all events he expected the coming of the kingdom of God and the eschatological judgment of the

10. The baptism of Christ. Painting by Piero della Francesca (c. 1415–91), London, National Gallery.

The **baptism of Jesus** by John the Baptist is now usually reckoned to be a historical event. There are different forms of rituals involving water in ancient religions, including Judaism. Alongside John's baptism, mention can be made of Jewish washings for cultic cleansing and proselyte baptism. The practice of baptizing people who revered Jesus as God's Messiah seems to have begun very early in the Jesus movement.

'Son of man', a being in human form who was entrusted by God with the judgment. Jesus' followers probably already thought in his lifetime that he was a Messiah ('anointed', i. e. the messenger of God who frees the people), the Son of man and God's son. Being 'God's son' similarly meant having been given by God a task for the people which was both religious and political, along the lines of Psalm 2, in which God declares that the king is his son.

The story of the temptation of Jesus by the devil follows the baptism and introduces the transition to the public activity of Jesus. It cannot be explained by asking the historical question 'Who was there to witness it?' But it does investigate further the question what the title 'Son of God' could mean. It does so in connection with the fellowship of Jesus' followers.

Jesus is led by the Spirit into the wilderness, where the devil takes the opportunity of meeting him alone and hungry after forty days of fasting. 'The devil says to him, "If you are the son of God, command these stones to become loaves of bread." But he answers, "It is written, 'Man shall not live by bread alone'"' (Matt. 4.4).

The dialogue with the devil is constructed like a dialogue between scribes, in which each side produces biblical quotations and argues with their help. Jesus' first answer to this challenge goes with the admonition 'Do not be anxious' in the Sermon on the Mount, which is about body and life, food and clothing (Matt. 6.25–34). The friends of Jesus, men and women, attempted to lead a hand-to-mouth life without cares or provisions, without being anxious about what the next day might bring. Jesus is not in principle against the kind of miracle that the devil proposes to him. In other situations he will feed thousands with a few loaves and two fishes. He does not argue for hunger or asceticism, but he does not want

In the dogmatic sense, the expression **Son of God** is understood to denote a unique being who unites in himself the divine and the human substance without mixing them. This late dogmatic interpretation contradicts the biblical usage, which regards God as the Father of all human beings. Paul speaks of Jesus as the 'firstborn among many brothers and sisters' (Rom. 8.29). In the Gospels the designation Son of God is not exclusive and christological but inclusive; it refers to the company of Jesus' disciples. Jesus understood himself as a Jew faithful to the Torah; he was not interested in the exclusiveness of the designation.

bread to have the last word, for it to be appointed lord over human beings and God. If the people of the Jesus community were to want or even stage such a miracle, they would no longer be orientated on God. They would accept the 'death by bread alone' which threatens so many people, particularly in the rich countries.

Here the devil is not just tempting the prophet from Nazareth as an individual soul. He is attempting to establish his lordship and power, to make them unassailable as a goal in life by suggesting that the means of life are life itself. This is a radical materialism, without spirit and soul, and the God who conjures up the bread is made an instrument to bring it about.

It is important for understanding this story to imagine the people who told it. The story is not just about the temptation of Jesus but about what threatens the community of his disciples: false dreams of a God who is ready to hear those masses of prayers and makes the right magicians or gurus available to answer them. That becomes even clearer in the second temptation.

'Then the devil took him to the holy city, and set him on the pinnacle of the temple, and said to him, "If you are the Son of God, throw yourself down"' (Matt. 4.5f.). Here the tempter takes up Jesus' method and uses a quotation from the psalms about the angels who 'will bear you in their hands' (Ps. 91.11) as the basis of an absurd proposal that Jesus should test God with a suicide attempt and suppose God to be available at any time. The matter-of-fact Jesus knows that God is not there to be tested. 'You shall not tempt the Lord your God' (Deut. 6.16). Thereupon in the third temptation the devil drops all his refined tricks and calls on Jesus directly to leave God aside and to found his own kingdom on his own

---

The **wildernesses** in the region of Palestine are not sandy deserts but limestone areas with a scattering of vegetation nourished by dew. This vegetation makes it possible for nomads to graze herds, especially in the winter. The proximity of the wildernesses to the narrow areas of cultivated land made migration and survival in the wilderness an everyday experience. The wilderness was regarded as a place of death, but it was also a refuge for the persecuted. It was the place where God could be experienced and where there was hope for God's coming to deliver the suffering people.

authority. He makes Jesus an offer of the kind of world rule that existed in the Roman empire and its order, which was idealized as *pax* (peace). For Rome, rule over the whole world was not only a daydream but reality. In exchange Satan requires only to be worshipped. Those who heard the temptation story and handed it on understood this to be an offer of power and rule in which there was no longer any talk of justice or mercy, the 'neighbour' or the kingly rule of God.

When Jesus rejects that, the devil gives up. But has he really given up? The most important interpretation of this

11. The temptation of Christ.
Painting by Duccio di Buoninsegna
(*c.* 1255–1319).

story, and one which takes it further, can be found in Dostoievsky's figure of the Grand Inquisitor, who gives the devil ongoing life. The son of God is executed by his own church. This church has entered into a pact with the devil because the way of Jesus was too hard for men and women and asked too much of them (F. Dostoievsky, *The Brothers Karamazov*, Book 5, Chapter 9).

3

Pax Romana: The Background to the Jesus Story

Hope for the kingdom of God, for an earth in which only God was king, was central to the messianic movements of Judaism in the first century. The expectation of God gave people power and imagination. Their resistance seized especially on the question of taxes for Rome. This was the consequence of the relationship to God: no human being any longer had the right to make claims on the body of another. But that is what the emperor did in Rome. He regarded the poll tax (*tributum capitis*) as the consequence of the conquest of peoples, so that their bodies no longer belonged to themselves but were the property of the new lord in Rome. This taxation of bodies was taxation of those without possessions, including women and children. From the perspective of many Jews, the acknowledgment of the emperor's lordship over men and women which was associated with the poll tax threatened to destroy their relationship with God. The rule in life for Jewish men and women was that God alone was to be lord and king, and no one else. Therefore the population vigorously grumbled about Roman taxation and suffered under it. However, we may doubt whether people in fact refused to pay tax on religious grounds. A refusal to pay tax would have amounted to open rebellion and have sparked off immediate military intervention by the Roman governor. But tension as a result of Rome's poll tax was in the air, and anyone suspected

---

Pax Romana

The emperor Augustus (ruled 27 BC–AD 14) boasted in his account of his actions (*Res gestae Divi Augusti*): 'I often waged wars all over the earth on water and on land against enemies both outside and within.' He listed the lands in a wide circle round the Mediterr-

anean as conquests of Rome: Gaul, Germania, Ethiopia and Arabia, Egypt and Greater Armenia. The consequence of these wars was the *Pax Augusta*, later also called the *Pax Romana*. 'Peace' meant that 'throughout the sphere of rule of the Roman people, on water and on land, an established

of resistance was also rapidly suspected of refusing to pay taxes. This accusation was also made against Jesus: 'We found this man perverting our nation, and forbidding us to give tribute to Caesar, and saying that he himself is Christ, a king' (Luke 23.2). This accusation is very probably false; however, it is true that Jesus regarded the tax as an expression of oppression by a foreign power (Matt. 17.25). Like all politically aware people of his time, Jesus suffered under the Roman demands for submission which time and again threatened Jewish monotheism. He thought it possible to pay the poll tax if it was clear to whom one's own body belonged: God alone.

Jesus made his first appearance in succession to John the Baptist. A consistent line runs through the brief period of his public activity. All the Gospels report how shortly before his arrest he was asked about the tax: 'Is it lawful to pay the poll tax to the emperor or not?' (Mark 12.14). The question was put by some Herodians and Pharisees. The questioners must have already disagreed with one another. The Herodians, probably above all royal officials, will have put forward the strict Roman standpoint. However, the Pharisees may have regarded the tax as an ungodly instrument of oppression, while nevertheless gnashing their teeth and paying it. Jesus then formulates the situation of the oppressed. They will have to pay taxes, but nevertheless must give God what belongs to him. They are not to grant the emperor power over their own bodies, even if he lays claim to them with the tax: 'Render to Caesar what is Caesar's, and to God what is God's' (Mark 12.17). This answer is often regarded as a diplomatic evasion on the part of Jesus. But such an interpretation fails to recognize the situation. On the one hand people were handed over to oppression; on the other they could hold fast to the liberating power of their God and put themselves at God's

peace has been introduced through victories'. This peace was celebrated as a golden age by writers devoted to the emperor in the time of Augustus and long afterwards. The tradition can still be recognized in German histories of the Roman empire. Contemporary critics of the *Pax Romana* gave a voice to those who had been subjugated. The British general Calgacus is cited by Tacitus (in *Agricola*). He said that the Romans were 'robbers of the world', insatiable in swallowing up lands. 'They falsely name theft, murder and robbery "rule", and where they create desolation they call it "peace".'

disposal. Jesus was not executed for refusing to pay tax but because he opened up ways of liberation for the men and women of his people in a situation of oppression. 'But human beings belong to God alone' was the comment of a Christian around 180 years later (Tertullian, *Scorpiace* 14). He got the point. What does it mean to belong to God—now—in our situation? This question accompanied the whole of Jesus' activity.

Even today it defines what it is to be a living Christian. People 'belong' to God, not in the sense that God is their owner but because he has created them—in freedom and for freedom. No father, no emperor, and no authority has the right arbitrarily to use people as things. This religious basis for human rights lies in the distinction which Jesus makes with the words 'what is Caesar's' and 'what is God's'. No one has the right to use others as 'bodies', as they please. All children today who are starving or who die from illnesses which could be cured 'belong' to God, and not to the lords of a global economic order which bears responsibility for the increasing hunger.

12. Statue of Augustus from Prima Porta, early first century AD, Rome, Vatican Museum.

The Jews were one of the peoples subjugated by Rome and politically were particularly unruly. Rebellions broke out time and again. Rome waged two wars against them, in AD 66–70 and 132–35. The temple in Jerusalem was destroyed in AD 70. From AD 135 Jews were no longer allowed to live in Jerusalem.

The origin of Christianity and the New Testament is part of Jewish history under the *Pax Romana*. The texts of the New Testament were written by Jews who had been subjugated by Rome and exploited economically.

What is Caesar's
A Meditation on Matthew 22.21 in the Gulf War
And what belongs to Caesar?
The bird its wings gummed up with oil
the sunless heaven in the stink
the hospitals without water
Yes, that belongs to Caesar
And the palace of the Emir Al Sabah
the gold on the doorknobs of all the bathrooms
the marble from Italy, the silk brocade
the US Army Corps of Engineers
who rebuild this castle for three weeks
so that now the sheikh is again free to bathe
Yes, that belongs to Caesar
and our taxation the eleven billions
the one hundred and sixty three marks of the woman
who knew nothing of it
Render to Caesar what is Caesar's.

What then belongs to God?
There were once birds
there were once clouds and water
the children without protection on this earth
do not forget that they belonged to God
one day there will be laughter
the work in the laboratory and our addictions
and our eyes, our hands
they will belong to God

We want to give to God what is God's:
the life of our brothers and sisters
and our hearts

Dorothee Soelle

The so-called Gentile Christians,
i. e. men and women of non-Jewish
origin who through their belief
that Jesus was the Messiah of the
Jewish people had opted for Judaism, along with other 'proselytes',
are also to be reckoned among
the Jews.

4

A Day in Capernaum

Capernaum lies on Lake Gennesaret, a couple of miles south of where the Jordan flows into what is often called 'The Sea of Galilee'. It was a small provincial city with a toll station; soldiers and officers of Herod were stationed there. Jesus was travelling round Galilee. He had left Nazareth, his home town where his family lived, and with it regular work and basic security. Here his new—short—public life began.

'So they came to Capernaum' (Mark 1.21). Jesus' first public appearance takes place in a synagogue on the sabbath. Jesus is a teacher, a wandering rabbi who interprets scripture and like any preacher translates it in terms of the present. He does so—in this first account of his activity—in a dramatically heightened form. A sick man, with a severe psychological dis-

13. The ruins of the synagogue of Capernaum.

order, interrupts Jesus with piercing screams: 'You have come to destroy us.' The man's fear for his own life, perhaps for the laboriously constructed order which this sick and wounded soul has made for itself, breaks out here. The frenzied man speaks with two competing voices within him. One belongs to the demon, who defends his territory, his power over the sick. He feels threatened and cries out: 'What do we have to do with you, Jesus of Nazareth?' (Mark 1.24). The other voice is heard by those gathered in the synagogue when the sick man, picking up words from the Psalms, says, 'I know who you are, the Holy One of God.' In the Psalm (16.10) the suppliant says to God: 'For you will not leave my soul in hell nor suffer your holy one to see corruption.' The hell of psychological misery is present in this healing story from Capernaum, and Jesus answers it by taking sides with the possessed man and driving out the 'unclean spirit'. Roaring in a frenzy, the sick man collapses, and the evil spirit 'departs'.

At that time sicknesses, above all of this kind, were regarded as the result of the power of evil spirits. Those in the synagogue understood the departure of the evil spirit to be a sign of the power of God alive in Jesus. Word and sign, teaching and healing, belong together.

Jesus

1
With a host of friends (women
    as well)
going through Galilee's villages
    and towns
he healed the sick and told stories
of the eternal God suffering in the
    world.

2
Privileges of class, education,
    were nothing to him
day labourers and tax collectors
    were among those around him
where there was a lack of food
    or drink
he distributed fish bread and wine
    to many.

3
The violence of rulers he scorned
to non-violent he promised the
    earth
his theme: the future of God on
    earth
the end of power of human beings
    over one another.

...

5
On a colt he came riding—the
    Messiah of little people
the fingers of a demi-mondaine
    completed his anointing
now confused now euphoric his
    friends the disciples followed
    him

14. The expulsion of the demon (above) and the banishment of the devil to hell. Decoration of the initial capital letter B in the twelfth-century Winchester Bible.

After this healing Jesus goes with his friends into Peter's house and there heals Peter's mother-in-law, who is sick with a fever (Mark 1.31). News of the miraculous unknown healer spreads like the wind, and the whole town gathers in front of Peter's house.

Jesus flees that same night and withdraws to a lonely place to pray there (Mark 1.35). His friends run after him and say 'They are all seeking you' (Mark 1.37), but Jesus wants to go further, through all the synagogues in Galilee. He wants to preach and heal; for him the two go together.

But Jesus does not do this all by himself. Even before the healing of the mentally ill man we are told of his quest for relationships. Jesus begins with friendships, with the formation of groups, with fellowship. He asks some fishermen to go around with him. They are to leave their old trade—sailing on the lake, fishing, casting nets, selling fish—and go with him to be 'fishers of men and women'. What Jesus wants

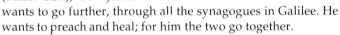

to sink perplexed into darkness at
    his arrest.

6
The swift trial rolled over his
    silence
an African took the beam for him
    to the place of execution

for hours he hung on the cross:
    torture with a deadly
    outcome—
three days later the unexpected
    change.
                                    Kurt Marti

requires fellowship, not a retreat into the wilderness. His message, which could be summed up as 'The time is fulfilled, the kingdom of God is near' (Mark 1.15), needs people who can be inspired by him and who already want to live with him in this dawning kingdom. This is no miracle which rains down on the people from above. Learning, travelling around together, becoming disciples, pupils, are conditions which are important for Jesus (Mark 1.16–20).

Why do they drop everything and follow him along the way? The accounts give no answer to this; evidently the attraction of Jesus, the air which he exudes, is so strong that justifications seem superfluous. Jesus and his friends rely on the people.

What is spoken of briefly here with reference to people who are mentioned by name is an ongoing process in the life of Jesus. The original Jesus community kept growing; it consisted of children, women and men who went around with him and with him got hungry and were filled, who found lodgings or remained homeless, were healed and became

Earlier research was concerned above all to extract the **'historical Jesus'**, purged of all later additions. In this connection the 'Jesus community' played only a minor role; the important question was whether the sayings of Jesus were 'authentic' or 'inauthentic'. In more recent feminist research and research into the social history of Christianity the questions have changed. The historical subject is no longer the individual hero with his allegedly absolutely 'new' qualities, but the community of brothers and sisters formed with and through Jesus.

The texts in which Jesus' words and actions have been transmitted have undergone a long process of oral tradition. In the Christian communities which came into being, time and again people kept telling the stories of Jesus. For them they were stories of how God comes to earth and also comes to them. They were treasuries of courage and hope. Only towards the end of the first century were the texts written down. So the character of the sources does not allow us to distinguish between 'authentic' and 'inauthentic' material. However, the social structure of the communities and their Christian lifestyle to some degree remained constant in these first generations. So we may conjecture that the tradition is very faithful and has preserved much of what Jesus said and did. Even this process of tradition still reflects that as a human being Jesus lived in relationships and cannot be isolated from his relationships with his friends, men and women.

In terms of content, each of the four Gospels has a very distinctive profile. In this book we attempt to respect these distinctive profiles and at the same time to recognize the traces of Jesus in the Gospels. However, for us the distinction between authentic and inauthentic tradition about Jesus in the first three Gospels is an outdated scholarly fiction. At the same time on theological grounds we do not regard the distinction as appropriate either for Jesus himself or for the people whose voices are heard in these texts.

healers, people who shared his life—and perhaps later also his death.

What supported them and what Jesus shared with them was God's indestructible nearness. Jesus' friends, men and women, already formed God's family here and now, a group

◀ 15. A fisherman on Lake Gennesaret.

not held together by blood ties or common features of nation, race or class. The people around Jesus are agreed that they will conform to the will of God in their lifestyle, their hopes, their actions and their suffering. Their common experience is that nothing is lost: hell does not have the last word.

5

Mary Magdalene

Mary Magdalene is present in the cultural awareness of Christianity as the converted sinner. She is often depicted with long blonde hair and great style, an erotic figure under the cross carrying a jar of anointing oil. This notion of Mary Magdalene has arisen as a result of referring several Gospel stories to one figure, although they originally dealt with different women and were not even connected with Mary Magdalene at all. Above all, the nameless prostitute (Luke 7.36–50)

16. Crucifixion, Isenheim Altar (1513–15). Painting by Matthias Grünewald, Colmar, Unterlinden Museum. The kneeling figure at the foot of the cross represents Mary Magdalene.

gives the iconographic tradition of Mary Magdalene her figure. Here we shall not be describing the later legendary tradition but the New Testament evidence.

Mary Magdalene came from Magdala by Lake Gennesaret, a small fishing port where fish were also processed. Like many of the women in the early church, she appears to have been unmarried. At any rate her name is not—as was customary—associated with a man's name, not even that of a father or a son. She must have been brought by Jesus into the prophetic group which formed in the fishing villages at the north end of the lake at the same time as Peter and some other fishermen. In addition to the name of Mary Magdalene we hear the names of Salome and 'Mary the mother of James the Less and Joses' (Mark 15.40). The texts say that the group of women was a large one: 'Now there were many women there (under the cross)' (Matt. 27.55; cf. Mark 15.41). These women disciples, some of whom were later also called apostles, went through the land with Jesus and the male disciples as prophetic healers and preachers. The way led from Capernaum to Jerusalem. In the Gospels they are usually simply thought of as being present and are not explicitly mentioned; this is a

consequence of androcentric language which mentions only men but includes women with them. However, this group of women takes on historical significance specifically in the events connected with the execution of Jesus in Jerusalem. The Gospel of Mark tells how the whole

17. A rock tomb like that in which Jesus could have been buried.

group of disciples fled when Jesus was arrested. The disciples were afraid of being arrested and executed with him. They fled in panic: 'And a young man followed him, with nothing but a linen cloth about his body; and they seized him, but he left the linen cloth and ran away naked' (Mark 14.50f.). The women, too, fled and hid in Jerusalem. When Jesus was executed by crucifixion they came out of hiding and cautiously dared to approach the dying Jesus. 'They watched from afar off' (Mark 15.40). They were—rightly—afraid, but they overcome their fear to the extent of not letting Jesus die alone. They then looked on as Jesus was buried in a rock tomb. The next morning they went to the tomb to honour the dead man by anointing his body with fragrant oil. In the eyes of the Roman rulers even respect for the body of an executed man was regarded as an act of solidarity, in other words as an expression of political disloyalty to Rome. The women slowly entered into this solidarity. Under the cross they stood far off, at the burial they looked on, and next morning they entered the tomb. They had overcome their fear.

Entering the rock tomb they saw the appearance of an angel. This angel commanded them to tell the other disciples that Jesus was going before them as the Risen One to Galilee (Mark 16.7). The women were terrified at encountering the radiance of God, the angel as his messenger, and the message that Jesus was

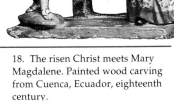

18. The risen Christ meets Mary Magdalene. Painted wood carving from Cuenca, Ecuador, eighteenth century.

risen. They fled from the tomb and 'told no one anything, for they were afraid' (Mark 16.8). The fear of God is again suppressed by the fear of Rome. Thus the Gospel of Mark ends with great dissonance: the men disciples have fled, the women disciples dared to go to the tomb, and now fear of Roman persecution again overcomes them. This dissonance arises out of the experiences of the people who handed on these stories. Their struggles with their own courage are reflected in the descriptions of Peter, the naked young man, Mary Magdalene and the group of women. In the first generations of the movement which was later called 'Christianity', the threat posed by Rome to any disloyalty remained the daily challenge. The dissonance at the conclusion of the Gospel of Mark is a silent invitation to the men and women in the community in whose assemblies and acts of worship the stories commemorating Jesus were read. They knew that Mary Magdalene and the whole group of women had then again overcome their fear, and that their bold appearance was the moment of the birth of the Jesus movement after Jesus'

death or—if we are careful about using the term—the hour of the birth of the church. In the Gospel tradition a group of women fighting with their fears founds a resurrection community in which people together seek and find the way of justice. In the eyes of the enlightened men of the Hellenistic-Roman élite these women were the worst witnesses

19. 'Noli me tangere'; painting by Rembrandt.

imaginable. Celsus, a second-century philosopher, mocked the resurrection community and the resurrection of Jesus: 'But who saw this? A hysterical woman, as you say, and perhaps some other one of those who were deluded by the same sorcery, who either dreamt in a certain state of mind and through wishful thinking had a hallucination due to some mistaken notion ... or wanted to impress the others by telling this fantastic tale, and so by this cock-and-bull story to provide a chance for other beggars' (Celsus, cited in Origen, *Against Celsus* II, 55).

Hardly anything is known of the actions of Mary Magdalene and the other women during the lifetime of Jesus. It is said that from the beginning they 'followed Jesus and served him ... and went with him up to Jerusalem' (Mark 15.41). This description presents them as disciples, for elsewhere in the Gospels, following, 'service' and the way to Jerusalem are also shown to be the characteristics of discipleship. In the Gospel of Luke there is a further special tradition: Jesus rid Mary Magdalene of seven demons—just as other women close to Jesus were healed of 'evil spirits and diseases' (8.3). Perhaps we can conclude from this that Jesus healed the sick from the beginning of his public activity (it should be mentioned in passing that we should not assume that the women were all mentally ill, since evil spirits were thought responsible for many diseases which today would be regarded as infections). This remark is important above all because it shows that after their healing, those who were healed remained in the company around Jesus. They were healed into a community. As the healing stories do not usually relate this continuation, if we are to understand them it is important to realize that they have it in view, even if it is not spelt out. At that time, in the communities this

Celsus of Alexandria was a philosopher of late antiquity. Basing himself on Platonic philosophy, but also influenced by the Logos doctrine of the Stoics, in 179 he turned against Christianity. He attacked in particular the Christians' way of life and their missionary practice. Celsus' work is known to us only through Origen's writings, in which passages from it are quoted. We know no details of his life.

continuation was taken for granted: the women who were healed became healers.

In later Christian tradition Mary Magdalene came to be identified with the nameless 'woman who was a sinner' (Luke 7.36–50). This story is about a prostitute. She arrived at a banquet uninvited. Jesus was one of the guests. She wept and washed Jesus' feet with her tears. Down the centuries this story has been read as the repentance of a whore. Prostitution was regarded as the fault of the prostitute. For her, Christian faith was meant to represent repentance for her guilt. No questions were asked about the social history of prostitution in the societies of the ancient world. History does not allow such an interpretation.

The rabbis, the teachers of the Jewish people, told of an unfortunate woman who wanted to save her husband through prostitution. Rabbinic teachers questioned a donkey-driver who could pray so effectively that he could even bring down rain: 'What good have you done? He replied: Once I hired out my donkey to a woman who began to weep on the way. I spoke to her: What is up with you? She replied: My husband has been put in prison and I want to see what can be done to ransom him (in other words she wanted to prostitute herself to earn the ransom). So I sold my donkey and gave her the ransom. I said to her: This is yours, redeem your husband and do not sin. They (the rabbis) said to him: You are worthy to pray and to be heard' (from the Palastinian Talmud, Ta'anith 1, 64b, 41). The imprisonment of members of the family for debt could also be a reason for prostitution.

Jesus' story about the 'woman who was a sinner in the city' does not mention the cause of her prostitution. This was

---

Prostitution was omnipresent in everyday public life, above all in the cities of the Roman empire. It was not thought disreputable for men to buy themselves women. Sexual intercourse between married men and prostitutes was not regarded as adultery. Women were almost forced to become prostitutes if they dropped out of the welfare system of a patriarchal family which functioned to some extent. A widow who had no resources and could not earn enough money to survive by her own work was compelled to prostitute herself— and her daughters. Such stories are

20. The master of a house exercises his *droit du seigneur* on a female slave—one of the numerous completely legal practices of sexual exploitation in the Roman empire. Wall painting from the House of the Vettii in Pompeii.

in fact an everyday experience for women and men, including the women around Jesus. The tears of the nameless prostitute should not be interpreted as a harlot's tears of repentance (as they usually are) but as tears of suffering from which there is no way out. Jesus turns to the woman as the donkey-driver turns to the woman in the story. She comes to him because she has heard that he can be found in the house of Simon the Pharisee. She hopes for healing from her suffering, liberation from her ongoing humiliation and the violence that she experiences. At the end we are not told that she will now

told again and again. Many women working in inns and taverns or in trade at the same time also worked as prostitutes. Child prostitution played a major role both for the children of slaves and also for girl infants who had been put out to die of exposure; they were gathered up for this very purpose.

travel on in the fellowship of the Jesus people, that she will no longer have to prostitute herself because others will share bread with her. That is so much taken for granted that it is presupposed. What is told, however, is how Jesus attempts to make her dignity visible in her life as a prostitute. For him she is not a bit of rubbish but a militant, suffering and loving woman. The love that she showed was not the harlot's love that men wanted from her but a love which brings God to earth.

The story of Jesus' encounter with this woman also contains restrained, even indirect, features of a story of the relationship between two people in which the love of God comes about. The women utters her cry for help with tears and gestures. At the same time she does Jesus a good deed. She lets her tears flow over his feet and dries his feet with her hair. She kisses his feet. Then she anoints them with precious fragrant oil which she has brought with her.

It was a custom to honour guests by washing and anointing their feet. What the host could have done in honour of Jesus is done by this woman, who has not been invited and has no water or towel. Jesus points this out to his host Simon, who is looking on critically. He may live more correctly according to the Torah than this woman who is a sinner, but she has shown him honour and great love: 'You gave me no kiss, but from the time I came in she has not ceased to kiss my feet' (7.45). She brought precious oil to anoint him with, but his host did not even anoint him with the ordinary oil used every day. 'Her sins, which are many, are forgiven (by God), for she loved much' (7.47). In her humiliation she had not lost the power of love which brings God to earth. She has fought, and it is an expression of her fight for her dignity that she has gate-crashed a banquet

Christianity is often called the '**religion of love**' and thus marked off from Judaism, which is associated with the 'God of vengeance'. At the same time the key phrase 'God of love' establishes a dualistic separation between spirit and body, heavenly and earthly, acts of God and human actions. The originally unitary understanding of love became increasingly polarized and was destroyed. The heavenly, merciful love of God which comes 'from above' was understood as *agape* (Greek) or *caritas* (Latin) and contrasted with *eros*, earthly love, orientated on desire and

21. The sinner with the jar of ointment— in Christian tradition often identified with Mary Magdalene.

uninvited in order to express her distress and her love for Jesus. Neither she nor Jesus nor the men and women who later handed on this story found the erotic nuances of the relationship between this woman and Jesus problematical. It was only later Christian contempt for the body which severed erotic love from the love which God makes human beings capable of.

pleasure. In the Jesus community the understanding of love has another function which a mediaeval hymn puts like this: '*Ubi Caritas et Amor, ibi Deus est.*' Where there is love in the full sense, there is God. It is this understanding of love that also characterizes the Hebrew Bible.

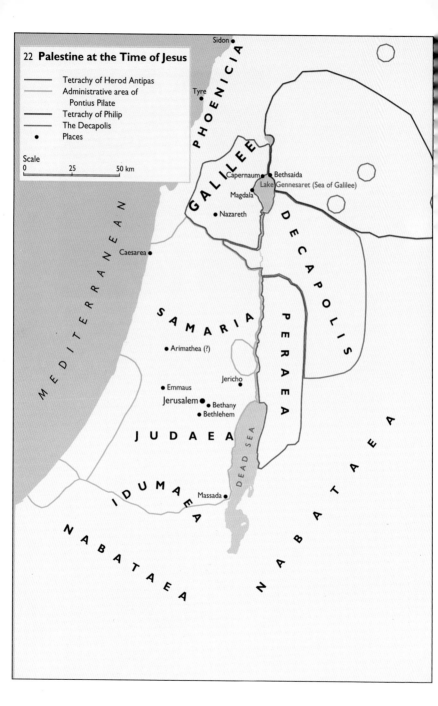

22 Palestine at the Time of Jesus

— Tetrachy of Herod Antipas
— Administrative area of
    Pontius Pilate
— Tetrachy of Philip
— The Decapolis
• Places

Scale
0   25   50 km

Sidon

PHOENICIA

Tyre

GALILEE

Capernaum • • Bethsaida
Lake Gennesaret (Sea of Galilee)

Magdala

• Nazareth

DECAPOLIS

Caesarea •

MEDITERRANEAN

SAMARIA

PERAEA

• Arimathea (?)

Jericho •

• Emmaus

Jerusalem • • Bethany
        • Bethlehem

JUDAEA

DEAD SEA

IDUMAEA

Massada •

NABATAEA

NABATAEA

6

Peter

At the beginning of his public activity Jesus called two brothers, Andrew and Simon, both fishermen, away from their families and jobs (Mark 1.16–18). Simon was later given the name Peter (derived from the Aramaic word Cephas); the Greek word *petros* means stone or rock. 'On this rock I will build my community', Jesus said to him (Matt. 16.18), after Peter had confessed that Jesus was Messiah and son of God. This new name and with it the authority of the keys, to bind and to loose, was solemnly bestowed on him. He was to hold together the Jesus community and time and again convene it; he was to lead it and guide it.

If we can speak of any understanding of office and leadership within the Gospel

23. Peter. Sculpture by Michelangelo on the Piccolomini Altar, 1501–4, Siena Cathedral.

tradition, it is based on this charge of Jesus to Peter and then later becomes clear in the first sermon which Peter gives in Jerusalem after Pentecost (Acts 2.14–36). However, there is a tremendous contradiction between this grandiose role of Peter as founder and leader of the church and another fact in the passion narrative which is told in detail by all four evangelists: the denial of Jesus by Peter in the court of the Jewish supreme council. Peter, the rock, the chosen and faithful one, several times confesses publicly that he does not know Jesus. Whereas the accused Jesus is mocked and struck and faces condemnation to death by crucifixion, Peter declares that he has nothing to do with him. 'I do not know this man' (Matt. 26.72).

This contradiction between Peter's commission, together with the promise that he had solemnly given earlier (Matt. 26.33, 35), and his actual behaviour touches on one of the deepest challenges of Christian faith. At the same time it is to the credit of the Christian tradition that Peter's denial of Jesus is not excused or suppressed, as is often the case in other heroic sagas. It belongs right at the heart of the Jesus story. The man who shortly before Jesus' arrest promises Jesus that he will die with him is the man who does not want to know his lord and friend and says that he has never known him. According to the various reports Peter is one of those who—in the language of the dark twentieth century—knew nothing, saw nothing and heard nothing: that is the meaning of the

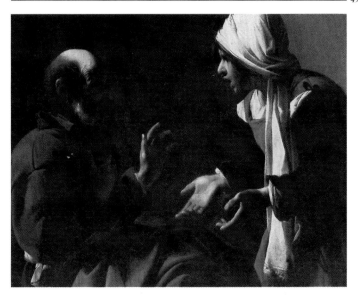

25. Peter denies Christ. Painting by a pupil of Caravaggio, early seventeenth century. Rome, Pinacoteca Vaticana.

legal term 'denial'. The one whom he wanted to follow, whom he explicitly regarded as the promised Messiah, is taken to prison, tortured and led to his death. There is Peter, the ardent friend of Jesus, time and again impetuous, the one who shares in the lifestyle of the Messiah—and Peter, the consistent and refined liar, who the moment he feels threatened and a potential victim of this new way of living declares all that he had experienced and hoped for null and void. The indication given by this confrontation of truth and lie, a vision of life in its fullness for all men and women, and an experience which brings with it nothing but difficulties, pain

◄ 24. One side of Peter: in defence of Jesus he cuts off the ear of the soldier Malchus. Relief in Naumburg Cathedral.

and torture, fear and death, belongs at the heart of faith. Here we can see what Christians experience, reflect on and have tried to live out under the heading of the great word 'cross', which is endlessly misused. The contradictory figure named Peter is an indication of the immense difficulties that had to be and still have to be expected by people who in the course of Christian history have committed themselves to the way of Jesus.

The slave girl who sees Peter standing in the courtyard and had already seen him in the company of Jesus and recognizes him by his dialect, as well, does not intend to betray him to the authorities, but is just engaging in conversation. Thus the motive for denial is given three times before the cock crows. Peter was not only the rock on which the church came to stand; he was also the one overcome by fear, who dropped out when things got serious. This contradiction is not left to stand, but in the New Testament itself is reconciled and healed in the bitter tears which Peter sheds when the cock crows in the grey dawn.

Like Peter, Judas, who presumably handed Jesus over to the authorities for reasons connected with his disappointment at Jesus' failure to intervene as the Messiah, desperately repented of having delivered up 'innocent blood' (Matt. 27.4) to those in power. We are told that he publicly acknowledged what he had done in a vain attempt to turn back

26. The suicide of Judas. Fresco by Pietro Lorenzetti, *c.* 1327. Assisi, basilica.

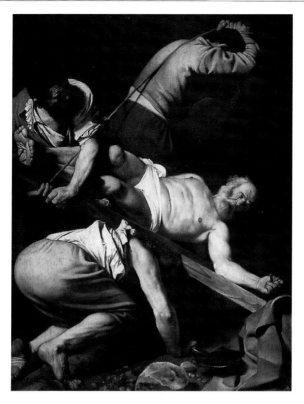

history. We hear nothing of the liberating bitter tears which are a sign of *teshubah*, the Jewish word for repentance. Judas is the tragic counterpart to Peter. He throws the reward he has been given at the feet of Jesus' opponents and chooses death by hanging. Peter took the Jewish way of repentance, which finally brought him to the cross in Rome. As late

27. The crucifixion of Peter, painting by Caravaggio, 1601. Rome, Santa Maria del Popolo, Cerasi chapel.

legends tell, he was crucified head downwards, in other words in such a way that he took longer to die.

Peter, Judas and Jesus died in what they attempted. The story of Peter's denial and tears corresponds to the stories of the flight of the disciples, who left Jesus alone, who slept when they should have been watching and praying. But the way that they show leads from the unfounded anxiety which John Chrysostom called the 'spell of fear' (Homily 85 on Matthew) to the new messianic practice of a shared and different life. The earliest church in Jerusalem, which was so important for the evangelist Luke, is the model of the way that people found out of the prison of fear by remembering Jesus. The men disciples, taught above all by the testimony to the resurrection by the women disciples, emerge from the prison of fear and hopelessness. It is no coincidence that the first to bear witnesses to Jesus' resurrection were not men but women.

In a sense the denial of Jesus Christ continues in the history of his churches. The Roman Catholic 'no' to women, to their vocation to ordination, to their dignity and their office as representatives of Christ, is an 'I do not know you', which the present-day Peter says to the living Christ.

7

The Blessing of the Children

The Jesus community did not just consist of adult women and men who had attached themselves to the man from Nazareth. In all pre-industrial society children are part of a poverty which is taken for granted. They were present when Jesus healed the blind or the lame; they came into the house when he was invited by others; they plucked ears of corn when they were tormented by hunger; they interrupted discussions; they whined and wept when they felt uncared-for or neglected. They were taken so much for granted that the accounts of the life of the original Jesus community which are given at length and with everyday realism in the Gospels make no mention of them. However, when it is said that 'many people' come to Jesus, there will have been children among them. They are just not noticed, taken heed of or even included in the count, as when in connection with the feeding of

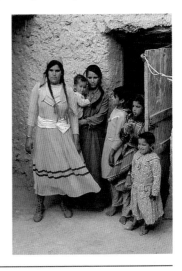

28. The life of children in rural Egypt today is still very like that of children in the time of Jesus.

crowds by Jesus 5,000 or 4,000 men are mentioned, but in three out of the four Gospels there is not a word about women and children.

According to the Jewish law of the time, parents had a duty to feed their children up to the age of six; after that the children had to fend for themselves. Here as also in many other questions we must imagine that the social situation in the towns and villages of antiquity was like the situation we know only from the accounts of the worst poverty in the present-day Third World: child labour in the fields and the workshops; begging, thieving and even prostitution; the selling of children into slavery, bands of street children as the only possibility of survival.

The story of Jesus and the children (Mark 10.13–16) presupposes this brutal situation and should not be confused with our often romanticizing idea of childhood: 'People brought children to him so that he might touch them.' The 'people' are women with infants and small children; the larger children accompany them. The disciples shout at the women; they want Jesus only to teach adults (10.1). Here Jesus acts like a pious Jew to whom children are naturally important. In the view of the Pharisees a lack of knowledge of the Torah was a hindrance to faith for children; it had to be remedied as early as possible, hence the tremendous zeal for learning and schools in Judaism. In Judaism, in the light of the creation story, the exposure of children, particularly daughters, which was largely customary in non-Jewish Hellenism, was forbidden, as was abortion.

Praise at a terrible Christmas time

When the rain fell on the red
  cloaks of the Santa Clauses
and they took sweets from their
  sacks
and the children clung to their
  harassed mothers
and cried 'for me', 'for me', 'me' in
  front of the department store

two boys were walking behind me.
'At home in Chile,' I could hardly
  believe my ears

'the Christmas trees are much
  bigger,
and Santa Claus brings along
  everything, lots of things.'

I turned round and saw a twelve-
  year-old with dark hair
he said in clear German to the
  blond boy
'everyone gets something, you see,
no one gets nothing, you see, no
  one.'

Jesus gets angry with his disciples and friends; he sees no reason for keeping the children away from him. 'Let the children come to me, do not hinder them; for to such belongs the kingdom of God. Truly, I say to you, whoever does not receive the kingdom of God like a child shall not enter it' (Mark 10.14f.). What is the meaning of this 'like a child'? In the context of the ancient world it means being a dependent without rights and possessions. Children belong among the 'last'; being like them is part of life with Jesus.

In the development of Christian piety, understanding of the saying 'Unless you become like children' is remote from this original sense. Centuries later, and under different social conditions, another aspect of being a child was discovered, which can be described as an openness to the new and the different, to mystical wonder; an openness which seemed part of life itself. This mystical interpretation came to be closely bound up with Jesus' blessing of the children. Matthias Claudius ends his 'Evening Hymn' with the verse:

Let us become simple
and here on earth
like children be pious and joyful.

Claudius was not so naive as to think that children are always lovely and well-behaved. Here he is speaking from the tradition of piety in the Psalms, which time and again invite the soul to rejoice, to be happy, to praise life and its creator, as it was originally capable of doing. Time and again we hear the words 'Praise the Lord, my soul', as if the soul being addressed were in itself too lazy, too sorrowful, too sunk into itself and too intent on producing and doing to be able to accept any gifts. To become 'pious' means to be capable of

This is a true story from
   Hamburg-Altona
and three reasons in one
for praising God
for the glory that no one gets
   nothing, no one,

for the angel in the anorak,
for the Chile that was.

For the Chile that will be.
                    Dorothee Soelle

perceiving the beauty and goodness of life. This living piety can be perceived time and again in children in their capacity for wonder, which is often expressed as a tendency to be distracted, but at the same time expresses a oneness, a harmony with God's good creation which is not purposeful. 'Receiving' life is the word which Jesus uses of the children: they do not have to produce it but simply to open their hands to be given it.

Here Jesus is not just expressing himself verbally. He puts his arms round the children, lays hands on them and blesses them. In many religions blessing is a custom which is expressed in gestures and few words, and also in silence or by lighting a candle for someone else who needs blessing. Behind it stands a basic religious awareness that we ourselves do not make life. The person giving the blessing shares the power of God with others and in the sacred action transfers power and protection to those who cannot bless themselves.

Blessing is a basic gesture of faith. In blessing people share with one another what they have been given; for those who are blessed this involves extreme passivity and an awareness that leaving and entering life are not in our hands, nor are they guarded by our troops! We do not just live by our work, our efforts and inventions, our productivity and our achievements. Vulnerable life needs another protection, another refuge, than what we can give one another. Perhaps children know more about that than adults who have often lost their religion in a competent life. Blessing and being blessed have something to do with losing one's self and finding a home in the ground of all existence, in God.

8

The Conflict over the Sabbath

The sabbath is the day of rest for the Jewish people. After six days' work one day is to be without work, when people are free to enjoy good food, to be together, free for the beauty of life and the praise of God. God himself has provided the rhythm of creation by working on it for six days so as then to rest on the sabbath. Even housewives can rest: the food is prepared the day before. The sabbath is festively welcomed with lighted candles, a shared meal and praise of God. To be able to praise God means to experience one's own body as created by God, to be able to eat one's fill and stretch one's limbs in happiness and fellowship. It pained Jesus that not everyone could praise God on the sabbath. He saw people being deprived of joy in the sabbath; he saw those who were hungry, unemployed, were worthless, and those who were

29. The sabbath. Painting by Isidor Kaufmann, c. 1920.

tormented with diseases and pains that completely took possession of them. God the creator wants all men and women to rejoice on the day of rest—so grief about the indignity of sufferings is particularly severe on the day of rest. Everyone should be able to praise God. In the Hebrew Bible 'everyone' includes men and women slaves; strangers with no rights and even animals are to take part in the sabbath.

The Gospels (Mark 2.23-28) tell how Jesus and his disciples went through the fields on the sabbath. The disciples began to pluck ears of corn and rub them in their hands so they could eat the grains. They were hungry. The scene was a public one. Jesus' friends meant themselves to be seen plucking the ears of corn; the Jesus people wanted to demonstrate the hunger of the majority of the population and not just their own. The plucking of the ears was meant to be provocative; in the stories about Jesus it belongs in the category of 'prophetic actions'. All the onlookers knew that one was not meant to harvest or prepare food on the sabbath. Some women and men from among the Pharisees thought that the Jesus people were violating the sabbath commandment. 'Why are you doing that?', they asked. 'It's forbidden.' Jesus sensibly replied to them: you can read in scripture what must be done when a commandment of God clashes with basic human needs. The sabbath is meant to make it possible to experience the dignity of human beings as God's creatures: men and women are meant to eat joyfully and praise God. Hunger is the destruction of body and soul. The sabbath means making the good news for the poor visible, capable of being felt and tasted. The hunger of the people must not be allowed to continue; it prevents or hinders people from praising God. It brings death.

The story of the plucking of the ears of corn has been widely associated with a pattern of interpretation which is

Pharisees

Even in the post-Christian societies of the Western world the term 'Pharisee' is a metaphor used frequently and thoughtlessly for 'hypocrites', especially for the so-called sanctimonious hypocrisy of publicly preaching water and secretly drinking wine. In the Christian tradition of interpreting the encounters between Jesus and the Pharisees these scenes are usually seen as 'controversies' in which the Pharisees put forward a 'legalistic' standpoint, i. e. one which is narrow and misanthropic, and Jesus shows them God's love. For Christian interpreters, after

30. A Pharisee. Book illustration, twentieth-century.

deeply established in Christian awareness. The Pharisees, who are identified with 'the Jews', are thought to have used the sabbath to oppress people. Hence Jesus' accusation, 'The sabbath is made for man and not man for the sabbath' (Mark 2.27). The second half of this sentence ('man for the sabbath') cannot be found anywhere in Jewish tradition; it is simply a rhetorical endorsement of the first positive sentence. Jesus' arguments with the Pharisees are meant to win them over, not alienate them. Pharisees and Jesus people are agreed in their evaluation of the sabbath.

The Pharisaic movement was made up predominantly of ordinary people. It attempted to shape the religious identity of Jewish men and women in everyday life. The typical picture of Pharisaism today should no longer be that of underhanded and gloomy opponents of Jesus but of a family which eats together and in so doing observes the regulations for cleanness in accordance with the Pharisaic interpretation of the Torah. Limestone cups have been found in excavations in many parts of Israel. According to Pharisaic teaching they were regarded as clean since—unlike clay and metal vessels—they could not be made unclean. Why did women and men attach so much importance to using such cups? In so doing they indicated very

---

such controversies Jesus leaves the stage as the true victor and embodiment of the Christian church, and the Pharisees seek to kill him. There are historical and theological reasons for criticizing this picture.

precisely that they loved the God of Israel and wanted to shape their lives in accordance with his commandments, not only in their heads but in everyday life and in their physical behaviour. What they ate and with whom they ate was important to them, and mealtimes were also times of prayer and gratitude for the goodness of creation. Pharisaism was not embodied by the gloomy opponents of Jesus but by the Pharisaic family at a meal, women, men and children. The existence of women Pharisees, who made an active contribution towards shaping everyday life (and not just as their husbands' wives) should no longer be overlooked. Paul's parents were both Pharisees, as was Paul himself (Acts 23.6). From the beginning, the Christian eucharist was the foundation of the new Christian community which was coming into existence. Without the Pharisaic legacy this form of community would not have arisen.

There were many controversies in Judaism in the time of Jesus. Jesus' controversies with Pharisees belong in this story of conflict. The Pharisees play no role in the narrative of Jesus' passion. They took no active part in his arrest, trial and condemnation. The conflicts between Jesus and Pharisees were controversies over important existential questions. Many Pharisees, both men and women, followed Jesus. The controversies turned on questions of everyday life, for example whether the sabbath can be celebrated if part of the population is suffering from massive hunger (this is what Mark 2.23–28 par. is about, see above, p. 58), or whether divorces instigated by males do not cause grief to God's creation (Mark 10.2–12 par.). In every case both sides argue on a common basis, the Torah: 'Have you not read ...?' (Mark 2.25 or Matt. 19.4). Both sides want to show convincingly that they are united on this common basis.

31. The emperor's triumph. ▶
Titus after the Roman victory in
the Jewish War in AD 70. Relief
from the Arch of Titus, Rome.

Jesus and his followers were at one with the Pharisaic movement on many questions, above all the question of the resurrection and the need for oral interpretation of the Torah. The Sadducees had a more fundamentalist attitude towards the Torah, rejected the resurrection and had an alliance with Rome. The Jesus movement and the Pharisaic movement also belonged together politically in those parts of the predominantly poorer population which felt that Roman rule was a violent rule which sought to destroy their lives and their religious identity.

A generation after Jesus' execution by the Roman army, in whose eyes his fight against hunger and poverty made him a political rebel, there was the long-feared catastrophe of the war between the Jews and Rome (AD 66-70). Rome wanted finally to subjugate the unruly Jewish people completely. The temple in Jerusalem was destroyed. This robbed the people of its centre, for the temple was the place of the presence of God. Now the Pharisaic tradition became the only foundation for a new form of Jewish life: the family at meal time which lives according to God's will and celebrates the presence of God in its everyday life. The Pharisees became leaders of a people which had lost all other institutions of leadership. There were controversies between this Pharisaic leadership and the Jewish-Christian communities, which were harsher than those between Jesus and Pharisees. The four Gospels were written

down around this time, using oral traditions from the time of Jesus. There are two historical levels in the Gospels, one superimposed on the other: the time of Jesus and the time after AD 70. Bitter words against Pharisees come from this latter time, put on the lips of Jesus, especially in Matthew 23. Here they are accused of hypocrisy, but their teaching is not rejected (Matt. 23.3). When we read the Gospels today we therefore have to discover from the texts how harsh the controversies were. But even in the time after Jesus, the Torah remained the common foundation for both sides. The controversy was a fight over the right way for the people to take in an extremely difficult situation, not the expression of an irreconcilable opposition. Without the Pharisaic heritage, neither Christianity nor Judaism would have found the way into the future that they discovered at this time. The shared meal is an abiding sign of this common foundation, even if the forms taken by the meal grew apart in the centuries which followed.

9

Healing the Sick: The Miracles

Alongside the prophetic words and actions of the fellow-ship of disciples, the healings of the sick play a central role in the Gospels. There were many sick people among those who listened to Jesus: 'And they brought him all the sick, those afflicted with various diseases and pains, those possessed by demons, epileptics, and the paralysed, and he healed them' (Matt. 4.24). This summary report is meant to make a typical statement about Jesus; time and again he is surrounded by the sick and helps them. Here the word 'sick' is to be understood in a very broad sense. It denotes all those whose bodies are impaired by illness and handicap and cannot cope with their everyday life, people who have pain in body or soul. There is often mention of blindness and bone diseases, the consequences of hunger and hard work.

In the ancient world, too, there was medical knowledge and there were doctors who were trained in it. However, the sick people around Jesus hardly had the money and the op-portunity to seek out such doctors. Mark 5.25 tells the story of a woman who suffers from chronic bleeding from the womb and has spent all her money on doctors, who were unable to help her. The majority of the population had no money for doctors; they went to sanctuaries which specialized in heal-ings. In Jerusalem at the time of Jesus there was a sanctuary of Asclepios with many pools in which the sick were put for a

---

A **miracle** is usually understood to be an event which breaks through the normal laws of the world as explained by science. However, miracle stories are attempts by ancient religions and their mythologies to explain real exper-iences of people who are healed. According to popular Christian under-standing they have to be 'believed' even in defiance of one's own intellect. This superstition is further intensified in the dogmatic tradition since miracles tend to be attributed only to Jesus and have come to be regarded as proof of his divine origin. Today their truth-content in terms of their social setting and practical religious significance should be taken seriously.

divine force to heal them. Asclepios was a Greek god of healing.

The people who hoped for healing from Jesus also relied on his capacity to hand on God's power. They had heard of this; he was known far and wide for it. He handed on the power of God through contact and through words. He made the sick his partners in the fight for the life of the children of God. Jesus' healings of the sick are an expression of his and their trust in God as the creator who wants their lives. Here, being healed means becoming a child of God or daughter of Abraham, or even becoming clean, becoming holy. In connection with this idea other early Christian traditions have the term 'temple of God' or speak of becoming the temple of the Holy Spirit. All these names for the healed body share the notion that God himself, God's power, God's spirit will dwell in men and women—not only in their heads but right through their bodies. Those who have been healed can be recognized by the fact that they can praise God. Those who are healed begin to sing; they stand up; they can hand on

God's power themselves. Their eyes become capable of recognizing God's power in the people beside them and in the trees. All at once they can see where the kingdom of God has already begun.

This healing has little to do with medical therapy and health as our Western society understands it; on the contrary, ancient scientific medicine, too, was nearer to the divine and popular medicine than today's medical practice. The idea of sickness and health that we learn in our society has a dualistic stamp. Those who are fully able to function are healthy; the doctor/engineer repairs the body which has broken down or checks the healthy body. Anyone who is incurably ill or handicapped disturbs the picture of 'normality'. Dying is a private matter and does not happen to normal people. Our Western notion of health bars access to the meaning of 'healing' as Jesus understands it. The term 'miracle' which is customarily used contributes more towards misunderstanding than understanding, and moreover hinders a perception of the miracles that really also exist in our secular world.

The people around Jesus experienced miracles and saw them with their own eyes. They did not need to 'believe' them. For them this word meant something quite different from holding remarkable events to be true. Jesus assumed that his friends could feed the hungry, heal the sick and raise the dead as he did. 'Heal the sick, raise the dead, cleanse lepers, cast out demons' (Matt. 10.8).

The Gospels speak quite naturally of false prophets who will do great miracles (Matt. 24.24 par.) We are told that Jesus could do no miracle in his ancestral town of Nazareth. God's power, which can change people completely, is not a private possession of Jesus. God can be experienced and we can share God's power between us. We can hand on divine power

◄   32. The lame man healed.
Fresco from the end of the third or
beginning of the fourth century.
Rome, Catacombs of St Peter and St
Marcellinus, Orpheus room.

33. Jesus and the woman with a flow of blood. Fresco from the end of the third or beginning of the fourth century, Rome, Catacombs of St Peter and St Marcellinus, Orpheus room.

through words and contacts: not only did Jesus believe in God in this way, but so too did his disciples. They and rabbinic teachers are said to have had such capacities to heal. The Jesus tradition even says that healing the sick is a duty imposed by God, just as it is God's commandment to give bread to the hungry and water to the thirsty. This duty to

Draft of another kind of Easter hymn

The earth is beautiful and lives easily in the vale of hope. Prayers are heard. God lives behind the next hedge.

Not a line in the newspaper about tower building. The knife does not find the murderer. He laughs with Abel.

protect one's neighbour's body is not interrupted even on the sabbath, although all are to rest from work then.

The story of the healing of a woman who is bent over double (Luke 13.10–17) and has been unable to stand upright for eighteen years points once again to the conflict within Judaism between the group of Pharisees and the group around Jesus. Both are concerned to do the will of God; both seek to recognize him in the here and now. This is a dispute over the *halakhah*, interpretation. Perhaps Jesus' emphasis is shaped more by the awareness that he is thinking, speaking and acting on and for those who are weary and heavy laden.

Jesus sees the women bent over double in the synagogue, calls her to him and pronounces that she is healed. He touches her with his hands. 'And immediately she stood upright and praised God.' The sabbath is there for God to be praised. There is inevitably a conflict with the ruler of the synagogue. He has the task of supervising the sabbath service. He thinks that a chronic illness can still be healed after the end of the sabbath day. Jesus says that to heal is as urgent as to assuage thirst.

> Then Jesus answered them and said, 'You hypocrites! Does not each of you on the sabbath untie his ox or his ass from the manger, and lead it away to water it?

The grass is unfadingly green as the laurel. In the rocket launcher the doves nest.

The fly does not buzz against the deadly glass. All ways are open. In the atlas the frontiers are missing.

The word can be understood.
   Whoever
says yes means yes and
I love means now and
for ever.

Anger is slow to burn. The hand of the poor is never without bread. Shots are stopped in mid-air.

At night an angel stands by the
   door. He
has ordinary names and
says, when I die:
Arise.

Rudolf Otto Wiemer

> And ought not this woman, a daughter of Abraham whom Satan bound for eighteen years, to be loosed from this bond on the sabbath day?'
>
> And as he said this, all his adversaries were put to shame; and all the people rejoiced at all the glorious things that were done by him.
>
> (Luke 13.15–17)

In this story the dispute over the sabbath finds a good conciliatory solution. Jesus has not defeated or devalued his critics with arguments, but won them over.

Compare him confidently with other greats
Socrates
Rosa Luxemburg
Gandhi
he can match them all
but it would be better
to compare him
with yourself.   *Dorothee Soelle*

10

Prophetic Actions

Prophets and prophetesses raised their charismatic voices in the course of the history of ancient Israel, confronting the people with God. Their message was conveyed not only by their voices but also by their physical behaviour: the way in which they dressed, even their food could become a means of expression. John the Baptist ate locusts and wild honey, the food of the Bedouins in the wilderness, since for him the wilderness was the place of hope and encounter with God. Jesus, too, understood himself as a prophet. He and the men and women with whom he allied himself dispensed with any baggage on their wanderings. They had no money with them nor the sticks which travellers normally took along so as to be able to defend themselves against wild animals and robbers. They had no sandals on their feet, no provisions and no change of

34. In the time of Jesus dangers to life and limb which do not exist today lurked in the wilderness. Ivory carving from Phoenicia.

shirt (*chiton*). They could be distinguished from ordinary travellers even from far off. They made themselves vulnerable and dependent on people in the villages and towns, expecting to be welcomed by them and given food and lodging. So they went into the houses and passed on their message: 'God is near. The people can attain peace if you rise up and work with one another for peace. Then Roman legions can no longer subjugate you.' They sat in the dusty market places and healed the sick. They trusted in the generous hospitality of their people. They trusted in God, who gave them the sovereignty no longer to be anxious about food and clothing. If their message was burdensome to some who preferred to go on living as before, they could also be driven out of houses and villages (Luke 10.10f.).

We are told how Jesus expounded scripture in the synagogue in Nazareth on the sabbath day. He was given the

If the prophets broke in

If the prophets broke in
through doors of night,
the zodiac of the demon
   gods
like a terrible garland
wound round the head—
rocking the mysteries of
the falling and rising
heaven on their shoulders—

for those long strangers to
   horror—

If the prophets broke in
through doors of night,
making the milky ways
shine golden
on their palms—

for those long sunk in sleep—

If the prophets broke in
through doors of night,
tearing open wounds with their
   words
in the fields of habit,

bringing in something quite
   remote
for the day labourer

who has long since ceased to wait
   in the evening—

If the prophets broke in
through doors of night,
and sought an ear as a home—

Ear of humankind
overgrown with nettles
would you hear it?
If the voice of the prophets
were to blow
on the flute bone of the murdered
   children,
breathed out
the burnt air of the martyrs' cry—
if it built
a bridge from the dying sighs of
   old people—

Ear of humankind
intent on petty listening,
would you hear it?
                              Nelly Sachs

scroll of scripture; he un-
rolled it and hit upon the
gospel of the poor in Isaiah:
'The Spirit of God is upon
me, because he has annoint-
ed me. He has sent me to
preach good news to the
poor, to proclaim release to
the captives and recovering
of sight to the blind ...' (Luke
4.18). Then he rolled the
scripture up again and gave
it back to the synagogue
servant. Everyone was looking at him. He said only one
sentence: 'Today this scripture has been fulfilled in
your hearing' (Luke 4.21). A
young man, unknown, un-
employed and completely
unimportant in the eyes of
those in power, stands up in
the synagogue in his ancestral town of Nazareth and

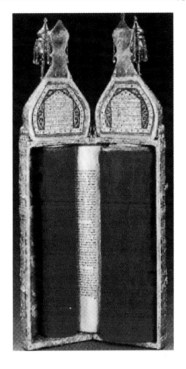

claims that the old promise of the gospel of the poor has been
fulfilled. He says that his own person is part of the liberation
which is now beginning. His voice creates a new heart and
new eyes. Prophets are not dubious soothsayers, but people
who name the truth for the present by name.

The remembrance of the history of the prophets of Israel
shows the way to the future; it is a power for the future. This
way of dealing with God's scroll has little in common with

35. A Torah scroll in a hinged con-
tainer of a kind customary today in
the East.

detached intellectual reading; it is a reading from which courage and power arises. Now, in this synagogue, people are changed. Jesus said that this way of reading scripture changes people's eyes, hearts, hands and feet. It is rather like what the prophet said when God gave him a scroll of scripture to eat: 'Then I ate it, and in my mouth it was as sweet as honey' (Ezek. 3.3). Dealing with scripture is itself a prophetic activity.

The theology which comes from the impoverished lands of the South offers a way which is often termed 'continuing to write the Bible'. In tens of thousands of communities, people, above all the rural poor, meet and discover the Bible as their ally. This new reading is done together and is usually embedded in a liturgical framework. Singing and prayer are part of the exegesis; the Bible is not 'studied', but people speak of 'praying the gospel'. Here they begin, not by worshipping the superman Jesus who can and will order all things, but by understanding themselves as his brothers and sisters. They themselves begin to tell one another miracle stories about being healed, about being filled, about another way of dealing with one another, and in this sense, two thousand years after the formation of the New Testament, they go on writing the book.

It is shameful that in the West an intellectual theology developed out of the tradition of Jesus which at the same time called for subjection under new 'scribes', a theology which made light of the reality of impoverishment and destruction experienced in the interest of the vision and hope of Jesus. Perhaps 'theopoesis' and 'narrative theology' of the kind that have come into being in many parts of the world of today are a better vehicle for narrating the acts of God. These acts are not summed up in doctrinal statements but describe the everyday life of women and men who live in and with Jesus.

Today this **living way of dealing with scripture** which changes people and illuminates their way is being endangered from two sides. One is literalism, which is a compulsion to declare particular events, relations between the sexes and dominant roles to be the 'Word of God' without any questions being asked and with no historical perspective. The prohibition against interpreting the text and bringing readers into another relationship with it than that of unquestioning obedience has held sway for too long.

The other danger is that of making the Bible superfluous by

Prayers of black slave women

Dear Massa Jesus, we all uns beg Ooner [you] come make us a call dis yere day. We is nutting but poor Etiopian women and people ain't tink much 'bout we. We ain't trust any of dem great high people for come to we church, but do' you is one great Massa, great too much dan Massa Linkum, you ain't shame to care for we African people.

Come to we, dear Massa Jesus. De sun, he hot too much, de road am dat long and boggy (sandy) and we ain't got no buggy for send and fetch Ooner. But Massa, you 'member how you walked dat hard walk up Calvary and ain't weary but tink about we all dat way. We know you ain't weary for to come to we. We pick out de torns, de prickles, de brier, de backslidin' and de quarrel and de sin out of you path so dey shan't hurt Ooner pierce feet no more.

Come to we, dear Massa Jesus. We all uns ain't got no good cool water for give when you thirsty. You know Massa, de drought so long, and the well so low, ain't nutting but mud to drink. But we gwine to take de munion cup and fill it wid de tear of repentance, and love clean out of we heart. Dad all we hab to gib you good Massa.

Harold A. Carter

One example of non-violent prophetic actions in the foot-steps of Jesus comes from the USA and took place in December 1999. Around 12,000 people followed the call of a Catholic priest, Roy Bourgeois, to take part in a major non-violent demonstration against the School of the Americas (SOA), a military academy in Georgia which since 1946 has trained around 60,000 Latin-American military. The aim of the academy was to combat revolts, make people disappear and torture them—in the last decade also using new kinds of torture which leave no trace. In 1996, as a result of the protests of many Christians over years, the school was forced to publish its handbooks, which provided compelling evidence against the murderers and their teachers. The group of protesters, which saw itself as Christian, and consisted above all of young people, whole school classes including students from

biblical scholarship which allegedly no longer needs any guideline or guidance. That the Word of God can be and will be 'a lamp to my feet and a light along my way' (Ps. 119. 105) is here dismissed as a naïve pre-scientific illusion.

But there is yet another, third way between fundamentalism and a belief that science has all the answers.

Boston Jesuit College, and also Dominican women from Houston and students of the St Thomas University in Minnesota, called for the closure of the torture school. They formed a funeral procession with eight coffins to recall the Jesuits murdered in El Salvador together with their housekeeper and her daughter; after that the names and ages of torture victims were sung in the style of a liturgy, for example, 'Maria Isabella, eight months old', or, 'the nameless child of Pedro Armarquez, eight days old'. After each individual name Lakora Indians beat their drums and then the crowd answered with the cry *presente* (Here, among us, present). The funeral procession penetrated military territory, bringing with it for 4,440 people the risk of six months in prison and a $5,000 fine. They took that into account—just as the original Jesus movement did.

11

The Sermon on the Mount and Love of Enemy

The Sermon on the Mount (Matt. 5–7) is regarded as the summary of what Jesus believed, taught and lived out. We have no written words from him, although there is historically good evidence that he read the scriptures. The later compila-

36. The Sermon on the Mount. Nineteenth-century painting.

tions of his words, which were certainly made only after his death, are the substance of what we can know of him. The audience is the circle of his disciples, men and women, but at the same time the Sermon on the Mount is a public speech to a crowd of people (Matt. 5.1), stylized as the speech of a king from his throne. It is the manifesto for the Messiah's government. The mountain is his throne, his words are inspired by God and the people is represented by the poor and the sick (Matt. 4.24). This king does not impose any heavy yoke of taxes or services (Matt. 11.28–30). He gives rest. He stakes his own life; he wants the healing of the people to begin with the hungry: 'He will not break a bruised reed or quench a smouldering wick, till he brings justice to victory' (Matt. 12.20, a quotation from Isaiah).

Jesus begins with words of blessing for the poor, in whom and with whom the kingdom of God comes into being.

> Blessed are the poor in spirit, for theirs is the kingdom of God.
> Blessed are those who hunger and thirst for righteousness, for they shall be filled.
> Blessed are the peacemakers, for they shall be called sons and daughters of God.

Beatitudes

He said:

I call blessed those who are poor. They are to live in God's kingdom. He also said: I call blessed those who mourn. They are to be comforted.

And we suppose

that this does not refer just to you and me but to our society as a whole and its ordinances. Which means that those who are in need, those who suffer want, those who lack anything, those who are thus interested in changing the world in the direction of the kingdom that is to come, those who grieve over the present distribution of land, education and knowledge, those who grieve over oppression, the withdrawing of the rights and the exploitation of two-thirds of all men and women—the promise is theirs.

He said:

I call blessed those who are meek: they shall possess the land. He also said: I call blessed the merciful, for God will be merciful to them.

And we suppose

that this does not refer just to you and me but to our society as a whole and its ordinances.

Here Jesus is not distinguishing between a blessing for his own followers and one for the people. He is blessing all who have become the 'light of the world' and hand on that light in the midst of the darkness of the empire. 'Light of the world' and 'salt of the earth' are demanding, indeed limitless, metaphors, which identify the inner theme of the Sermon on the Mount. Those who hunger for righteousness and are persecuted as a result are examples and models of how people will learn to praise God, how they will become 'blessed'. The definitions of happiness or bliss contained in this text do not distinguish between 'now' and 'later', between 'here' and 'there'. When the light of the world, which all can become, shines, those who perceive it learn to praise God (Matt. 5.16) and hand on this capacity. People rise up out of the hopelessness which cannot love God and therefore cannot praise.

This popular rebellion will be a different kind of rebellion, without hatred and the death wish. The rebels will love their enemies. Jesus does not speak here as a new Moses but interprets scripture for his day: 'You have heard that it was said by God, "An eye for an eye and a tooth for a tooth." But I say to you, Do not resist one who is evil. But if anyone strikes you on the right cheek, turn to him the other also, and if anyone would sue you and take your coat, let him have your cloak as

Which means that a group, a people which lives among its neighbours without aggression and without thinking in terms of friend and foe, which does not allow itself to be provoked and is not keen on getting at all costs what it regards as its rights—which on the contrary transcends the law and abandons a legalistic mine and yours—the promise is theirs.

He said:
I call blessed those who hunger and thirst for righteousness, for God will see that they are full. He also said: I call blessed those who suffer persecution for righteousness' sake, for their reward will be great.
And we suppose
that this does not refer just to you and me but to our society as a whole and its ordinances. Which means that those who try to create justice, to collaborate in constantly improving legislation and the penal system, a fairer distribution of property, an order of partnership between men and women, adults and children, teachers and pupils, colleges and students, employers and employees—and who for such efforts towards justice are defamed and suffer discrimination in their profession, their income and their freedom—theirs is the promise.

Vilma Sturm

well; and if any one forces you to go one mile, go with him two miles. Give to him who begs from you, and do not refuse him who would borrow from you' (Matt. 5.38–42). Here the every-day experiences of violence are mentioned: male and female slaves, free agricultural workers and day workers—they are struck and goaded on at work. Before those who are in debt come to court, even their clothing, their last tunic, is pawned. According to the Torah, only the upper garment may not be pawned, because it is at the same time the poor person's blan-ket. The Roman army conscripted people for forced labour, for example in transporting baggage. The impoverished could no longer get credit to buy seed and could no longer till their fields. This destroyed the subsistence economy. Jesus teaches a strategy of resistance which does not consist in hitting back but makes the injustice of violence visible: offering the other cheek, going out naked from the hall of judgment, not grum-bling when doing forced labour for a soldier but keeping him company on the way. Anyone who can should show financial solidarity with those who lose their land through debt. Fur-ther experiences of violence can be added. Jesus did not want to be perfect but to offer a form of resistance which makes violence in everyday life visible with simple means and inter-rupts it.

There are other strategies for women who experience violence and who are not mentioned here, as is told by a parable of Jesus (Luke 18.1–8). If they suffer injustice from creditors and judges they are to behave stubbornly and tena-ciously, to keep coming back if they are dismissed, and to cry loudly. At that time crying out was already a possible way for women to offer public resistance.

Jesus says: 'You have heard that it was said by God, "You shall love your neighbour and hate your enemy. But I say to

Love of enemy does not mean denying that people are hostile towards those weaker than themselves and acting as if there were no enemies of life. The starving children of this world, the fish, the trees, have real 'enemies', and Jesus would completely agree with Bertolt Brecht when he says:

'Evil has an address. It has a telephone number.' His people, the Jewish people, were oppressed by Rome. Love of enemy also means attributing to the enemy a capacity to repent, to change his or her mind, to behave differently. Love does not ignore hostility but makes people capable of overcoming it.

you, Love your enemies and pray for those who persecute
you, so that you may be sons of your Father who is in heaven;
for he makes his sun rise on the evil and on the good, and
sends rain on the just and on the unjust"' (Matt. 5.43-45).
Here too Jesus understands his preaching as the exegesis of
scripture, as making God's will present in a new situation.

Roman courts attempted to break resistance, usually by
passing death sentences. The 'ethic of Jesus' culminates in love
of enemy; enemies too have been created by God and have
'something of God' in them, this dream of another life without fear and hunger, in that happiness which is a response to

37. Convincing the enemy instead
of fighting him: Christ before the
high priest. Painting by Gerrit van
Honthorst, seventeenth century.

God and responsibility for the world. 'You are to be perfect as your heavenly Father is perfect' (Matt. 5.48).

Jesus' behaviour during his own condemnation demonstrates what love of enemy looks like in practice. He also delivers his message to his accusers: 'I am son of God'—loved and commissioned by God. The title 'son of God' is not a title unique to Jesus but an interpretation of what the Jewish tradition calls 'imitating God', who makes rain fall on the just and the unjust. If we read together both Jesus' response at his trial (Mark 15.62) and the command to love one's enemy, it is evident what it means to be son of God. We cannot discover historically whether Jesus also said before the court that he was the Messiah, king of the Jews (for example Mark 15.2 before Pilate). But at any rate he demonstrated the political consequences of his resistance. That is why he was executed.

We also know from the history of the trials of Jesus' followers that they overcame their fear before the courts and attested God's loving-kindness to their accusers. The judges who stood in front of them inflicted unjust state violence; they were enemies of God. Jesus countered them with an attempt to change them, too, into sons of God; he attempted to make it clear to them that oppression and violence were unjust ways that they could abandon. At that time people were fond of telling stories about the conversion of executioners. At the execution of Jesus, too, the commander of the soldiers who crucified him spoke the word of liberation: 'Truly this man was God's son' (Mark 15.39).

12

Shared Joy, Shared Bread: The Meals

In the Jewish tradition the shared meal takes a religious form. The head of the family or the host speaks a blessing over the bread at the beginning of a meal: 'Blessed be thou, Eternal One, Our God, king of the World, who bringest forth bread from the earth.' Then the bread is broken and all get a piece. This blessing hallows all the food on the table. The food is part of the ongoing creation in which people take part by

38. The Seder Meal. Popular Jewish water-colour from western Ukraine, nineteenth century.

eating it—and also through their work. Table fellowship is deliberately demonstrated as fellowship in actions like sharing the bread. After the meal the cup with wine is blessed like the bread and handed round. The form of the meal and the fellowship at table thus express thanks and praise for God through prayers and symbolic actions.

Jesus saw organizing fellowship meals as part of his divine task. He ate with those who were on the margins of society: cheats and prostitutes, toll collectors, all members of 'disreputable professions'. He ate with those who 'followed' him: men, women and children. He accepted invitations to meals in the homes of Pharisees precisely because on some individual questions relating to the required loyalty to the Torah he thought differently from many Pharisees. There were discussions and friendly disputes at the meals. At one meal Jesus allowed himself to be touched by a woman who was a sinner; the host, a Pharisee, found this intolerable (Luke 7.39). He accepted invitations to the houses of tax collectors: members of the Pharisaic movement would probably have refused them. They thought that careful observance of cultic cleanness in everyday life would help to safeguard their Jewish identity against threats. Behind

39. The Last Supper. Depiction from India in the time of the Mogul rulers.

40. The breaking of the bread as ▶ a sign of recognition also after the resurrection: The Meal in Emmaus. Painting by Rembrandt, 1648.

the term 'sinner' lies a mixture of demarcations on a cultic and social basis; for example there were professions which made people unclean because in them contact with the dead bodies of human beings or animals was unavoidable (for example grave-diggers and tanners). Jesus did not fundamentally question commandments about cultic cleanness. Like the prophets of the First Testament, he already combined cultic cleanness with a vision of fellowship in which all men and women, the people, humankind, would sit at God's table. This vision of the feast of the peoples in the kingdom of God, in which even all the homeless would take part, runs through his actions. God's banquet is depicted as a meal with an abundance of food created by God. The itinerant prophets, who were often hungry, and the undernourished men and women who shared the table with them, elaborated this vision and managed to experience together the fullness and the wealth of creation because they shared their bread, vegetables and wine.

This experience of the wealth which arises out of sharing is reflected in two traditions which scholars consider to be

historically different: first in the charge made by Jesus' critics
that he was a glutton and a drunkard (Matt. 11.19). From the
standpoint of the Pharisees, who were concerned with cleanness, Jesus' open dealings at mealtimes, derived from the real
situation of the hungry majority, were not 'correct' in either
religious or political terms. Jesus and his followers celebrated
popular festivals in the midst of the impoverished people.
They celebrated the vision of the banquet for the people in the
kingdom of God in the empty fields of Galilee. They opened
up ways which took people from their lonely struggle into
fellowships of sharing and justice.

At the core of the Gospels are the many stories of how
Jesus filled thousands with a few loaves and fishes. These are
not to be read as historical facts, but as visionary narratives
arising from what was in fact the realistic experience of happiness granted to the people around Jesus.

Five thousand people were fed with five loaves and two
fishes, and there was still something over. The story as related in the Gospel of Matthew says that there were 5,000 men,
'not counting women and children'. So might there have been
10,000 or 15,000 people? All the Gospels relate this miracle
with the loaves, and the Gospels of Matthew and Mark even
tell of two miracles with loaves, one with 5,000 and then one
with 4,000. These stories cannot be read as records containing

reliable numbers. The high numbers are meant to express that the fullness of the kingdom of God could be experienced around Jesus. Experiences are reflected in these fantastic stories. If a population which for most of the time is tormented with debt and the fight for survival tells itself such stories, it gives itself courage to build up communities of sharing. The more fantastic the numbers of the recollection of the experience of the kingdom of God become in Jesus' presence, the clearer the goal of his action also becomes: we too can share and experience the happiness of the kingdom in fellowship.

At the feeding of the 5,000 Jesus asked the people to sit down in groups of hundreds and fifties. This scene deliberately recalls the people in the wilderness when Israel was fleeing from Egypt before Pharaoh (Ex. 18.21, 25). The exodus tradition was about leading the people; here in the narrative about the miracle with the loaves, eating and fellowship in manageable groups stand in the foreground. Even if the

42. Two fishes and five loaves with which Jesus fed the 5,000. Early Christian floor mosaic from Tabgha, where according to legend the multiplication of the loaves is said to have taken place.

◀ 41. The feeding of the people of Israel on Sinai with manna. Mediaeval woodcut.

details of these stories are legendary, we can still recognize that from the beginning Jesus helped to build up communities which were responsible for each other, which prayed and ate together. They are the beginning of the form of life in communities (*ekklesia*), the beginnings of what later came to be called 'church'. The Christian eucharist arose out of such shared mealtimes.

The beginning of the eucharistic tradition can be found in Paul's first letter to the community in Corinth (I Cor. 11.17–34). The accounts of the Lord's supper in the Gospels were written later, but—with small divergences—reflect the same tradition. Paul reports:

> For I received from the Lord what I also delivered to you, that the Lord Jesus, on the night when he was betrayed, took bread, and when he had given thanks, he broke it, and said, 'This is my body which is for you. Do this in remembrance of me.'
>
> In the same way also the cup, after supper, saying, 'This cup is the new covenant in my blood. Do this, as often as you drink it, in remembrance of me.'
>
> For as often as you eat this bread and drink the cup, you proclaim the Lord's death until he comes.

An open letter to Jesus of Nazareth
Excuse me for writing to you.
I'm sure you know nothing about me.
I'm an insignificant case, Segundo Lopez Sanchez,
a carpenter by trade, married with five children.
I work for a building firm and do other jobs on the side.
I'm one of your poor.
For that matter, I've neither strength nor patience.
Lord, the battle for survival is a big one,
and the drink isn't enough.
Lord, it would be better for you to come down
and see it all with your own eyes.
I'm not very educated, but they say
that in your youth your practised the same trade as me.
I don't know what it meant at that time
to live by one's work and be poor.
But today it's a miracle,
greater than the one with the loaves and fishes,
if one can put anything at all on the table

> Whoever, therefore, eats the bread or drinks the cup of the Lord in an unworthy manner will be guilty of profaning the body and blood of the Lord (I Cor. 11.22–27).

The occasion for this account of the Lord's supper in Paul was a dispute in the community in Corinth (around the middle of the first century). Rich members of the community did not want to sit at the same table as the poor and share their food. Paul's account of the supper takes us historically very near to the time of the death of Jesus and the first supper. Paul says that he has received this tradition, presumably at the beginning of his conversion from being the persecutor of the messianic Jesus groups to being a passionate member of them. That must have happened a few years after the death of Jesus. In this report Jesus assumes the role of father of the family. He speaks the words of blessing which Jews take for granted as part of any shared meal. He shares the bread and adds the remembrance of his death to the prayers of blessing. The remembrance is to remain alive as a source of hope for the imminent kingdom of God 'until he himself comes'. Jesus comes as judge. Then God's righteousness will reach the whole earth. That is the hope of the community of remembrance at its shared supper.

and share so that everyone gets a bit.
You can experience that for yourself:
come and work as a carpenter with us,
try to get by on the daily wage.
You'll sweat blood, like that time in the garden.
Go on to the streets and begin to preach
as you once did against the Pharisees.
Repeat what you said about the rich
and the eye of a needle.
Drive the merchants out of the church
and we'll see what happens.
If they don't crucify you as they did then,
it will be because today a word is enough
to put you to silence. Isn't that a joke?
Lord, come and help us, so that they don't say:
'Even Christ can't solve the problem.'
Worker to worker, I ask you, and sign myself:
Your humble follower Segundo Lopez Sanchez.
Antonio Reiser and Paul Gerhard Schoenborn

The organization into manageable groups ('communities') and the community's expression of itself in shared meals ('the supper') was the foundation for the Christianity that was beginning. At this time and still long afterwards of course the Christians (= Messians) remained part of Judaism. Only with their departure from Judaism did the 'supper' too become disembodied. All that was left was symbolic food, and the body of Christ had little to do with people's real bodies. But time and again in church history women and men have done away with the disembodiment of the tradition and linked up with the actions of Jesus.

43. The Last Supper. Painting by
Leonardo da Vinci, 1495–98. Milan,
Santa Maria delle Grazie, refectory.

13

God in Everyday Life: The Parables

Jesus told parables, little scenes from everyday life or more dramatic stories about life. These parables spoke of human life and at the same time of God. In them everyday experiences became a window through which God could be seen.

Here is a way of speaking about God without mentioning God as agent or speaker; it is one of the basic forms in which Jewish tradition expresses itself. The richness and everyday realism of the parables are what give them their beauty. Here it is evident that in the Judaism of Jesus' time—as well as long before and afterwards—there was a living culture of telling parables. This was how everyday life was described and analysed; this was how people talked about the God who, Jews believed, communicates himself and whose will is known. 'It has been told you, O man, what is good and what the Lord requires of you' (Micah 6.8). It can be known, and the parables help here because they are so rooted in everyday life, and at the same time transcend it in a surprising way.

The openness of the parables, which do not nail anything down, is directed towards people who listen, reflect and then seek common ways with others. At that time those were ways of poverty and humiliation. The connection between individuals and the people as a whole is always presupposed. In the parables Jesus described the world of his experience, the world of the great estates which were administered by lease-

Behind the monastery
Behind the monastery. down by the road,
there is a cemetery of worn-out things
where lie smashed china, rusty metal
cracked pipes and twisted bits of wire,
empty cigarette packs, sawdust, corrugated iron,
old plastic, tyres beyond repair;
all waiting for the Resurrection,
like ourselves.
Ernesto Cardenal

holders, and the world of the day labourers and hard-working women.

One of the parables (Matt. 20.1–16) relates an everyday scene from the working world of a kind that can still be observed in the cities of the Middle East. Early in the morning unemployed men gather in the market place and wait for stewards or craftsman who are hiring day labourers for the working day that is beginning. A landowner wants the grapes picked in his vineyard, typical seasonal work. We can read in Roman textbooks on agriculture that in regions plagued by malaria the economically-minded employer will have seasonal work and work in the fields done by day labourers and not by slaves. He has to buy slaves, and must be interested in their further capacity for work. By contrast, day labourers are slaves at their own risk. They are born free, yet in an economy based on slavery their living conditions are even more miserable than those of the slave. Jesus and his followers, who kept telling one another this parable, had very precise knowledge about the working conditions of day labourers,

presumably also from their own observation. For they too were among the landless whose grandparents could still live on produce from their own fields, but whose parents had already succumbed to economic pressure as a result of the concentration of land ownership in fewer and fewer hands.

The parable notes all the important details. First of all the landowner hires men for the whole working day from dawn to dusk. He concludes a contract by mentioning the sum they will be paid and shaking hands. The day labourers know that they will be paid in the evening because the Hebrew Bible requires this of the employer, and most employers observe this law. The text tacitly presupposes that the one denarius is something like the minimum subsistence level; however, one may ask whether it would also feed the labourer's wife and children. The text says nothing about this. The employer in Jesus' parable then hires further labourers in the course of the day, at nine o'clock, noon, three o'clock and five o'clock in the

45. The wine harvest in ancient Egypt, relief.

◄ 44. A Roman farmhouse.
Wall painting from Trier,
c. AD 200.

afternoon. Those hired last have only around an hour's work ahead of them; then the sun will set. The landowner does not mention any sum of money to the second group, but indicates only that he will pay them a fair wage; he does the same with those who are hired late. The last group can hardly expect money—perhaps a portion of grapes. This way of hiring day labourers for parts of the day is meant to ensure that not too many labourers are hired. The employer calculates in stages the amount of work still to be done in his vineyard, which is evidently a large one. That is all the more remarkable since at this time work was not yet divided into hours or paid by the hour. The parable depicts a landowner who calculates very precisely and sparingly so as not to lessen his profit from the harvest by paying excessive wages. The pressure on the labourers to work quickly and effectively can be recognized from the procedure. Moreover the second part also mentions a steward who supervises the work and pays out the wages. That is how the evening scene is described. But the employer has completely changed his attitude. He is now unrecognizable.

> And when evening came the owner of the vineyard said to his steward, 'Call the labourers and pay them their wages, beginning with the last, up to the first.' And when those hired about the eleventh hour came, each of them received a denarius. Now when the first came, they thought they would receive more, but each of them also received a denarius. And on receiving it, they grumbled at the householder, saying, 'These last worked only one hour, and you have made them equal to us who have borne the burden of the day and the scorching heat.' But he replied to one of them, 'Friend. I am doing you no wrong; did you not agree with me for a denarius?

Take what belongs to you and go; I choose to give to
this last as I gave to you. Am I not allowed to do what
I choose with what belongs to me? Or do you begrudge
my generosity? So the last will be first and the first last'
(Matt. 20.8–16).

The employer pays everyone the full day's wages, regardless
of how long they have worked. He sees that even those who
are unemployed and found little work need the denarius,
their survival wage. We should not overload this parable of
Jesus by treating it as a detailed social and political pro-
gramme for his time or for ours. In paying the wages the
landowner is going by people's needs, not their achievement,
although he would have had the right to pay far less. Those
who have worked a long time protest, because they have not
or have not yet undergone the same change as the landowner.
The ending of the parable is an open one, with the wordless
invitation of the employer to those who have worked a long
time to open their hearts and grant the unemployed the
denarius they need to survive on.

This is an everyday scene, but in the evening all at once
different laws prevail from those during the day, in a society
orientated on profit. The employer changes his behaviour
completely. Not a word is said about God. Only the introduction to the parable mentions God: in what follows there is
mention of the kingdom of heaven, of the laws of action when
God and no one else is king on the earth. The parable trains
its hearers to see the misery of the unemployed. It describes
the pressures of an economy orientated on profit and the
victims of this economy who stand unemployed in the market
place from six in the morning to five in the evening, still waiting. The parable makes room for the notion that change is

◀ 46. Three of the earliest
coins minted in Palestine,
first century BC.

Jesus Christ

In the Indio we see Jesus Christ suffer, in the Black we also recognize his face,

he is in them, shares their poor life, on the edge of society, outcast.

He bears the features of all the countless who live as dependents with no land of their own,

handed over to the whim of rich masters, who without scruple exploit their work.

He is among us but we know him not; he is here among us, yet we despise him.

He walks in the figure of those bowed down, who do hard work for bad pay,

who toil for others with almost no rights, no voice, in order to survive.

Who live packed together in the poor districts, victims of hunger and sickness

and painfully within sight of all the wealth and extravagance of the thoughtless.

He is among us but we know him not; he is here among us, yet we despise him.

We see Jesus Christ in the many who can barely live without work,

who are victims of economic action, who heartlessly think only profit and power important.

We also see him in all the young people who have no possibility of learning,

who without work or orientation succumb frustrated to the intoxication of drugs.

He is among us but we know him not; he is here among us, yet we despise him.

We also see his face in the children, painfully lined by merciless hunger,

abandoned, helpless, without support, fighting for life without their parents' protection.

The old too bear his features, an image of their joyless life,

despised, useless, sick and misunderstood, cast out of the world of others.

He is among us but we know him not; he is here among us, yet we despise him.

I was hungry and thirsty as a beggar; in rags I went sick and homeless.

Persecuted, banished, arrested, imprisoned, I suffered all the torments of my brothers and sisters.

Blessed are those who find me in them, who accept me into their hearts, their lives,

they will find a home in the kingdom of God. Come to me, I am waiting for you to come.

He is among us but we know him not; he is here among us, yet we despise him.

Author unknown

possible. The employer changes his orientation on profit, and those who work for a long time are invited to show solidarity. The parable is sparing with indications of any conclusions that are to be drawn. It presupposes that those who relate and hear this text will together find a way to establish justice in small steps—as the employer indicates by his behaviour. The parable is even more sparing with words about God. The people who related or heard this text at the time were familiar with the scriptures and they knew the Psalms. 'Merciful and gracious is God, long-suffering and of great goodness' (Ps. 103.8) echoed in their ears.

We know from the history of early Christianity that there were more women than men in the communities. They do not make an appearance in the parable; that is on the one hand because of the androcentric, i.e. male-centred, language which quite often tacitly includes women, and on the other hand also because of the way in which the working world was organized. In fact only men would have stood in the market

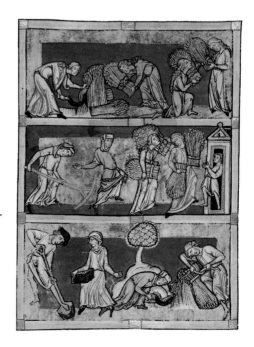

47. Women working in the fields. Book illustration from the *Jungfrauenspiegel,* twelfth century.

48. In Egypt men, women and children help in winnowing the grain.

place in the morning. But the denarius, the day's wages, was not enough for the family. Women, even married women, had to do domestic work to earn money. They were paid less than the male day labourers: for work in the fields they received less than a denarius a day. They were given hard work, and their search for work was less of a public one. Perhaps they would be allowed to weed the vineyards. Women were employed to help in agriculture and to work in the newly developing textile industry. They had to work outside the house in order to contribute towards supporting the family. It was impossible for lower-class women to lead an economically independent life.

There is a parable of Jesus which can be read as a continuation of the parable of the labourers (Luke 15.8-10):

49. Joy at finding the lost ▶
drachma. Painting from the
nineteenth century.

... or what woman, having ten drachmas, if she loses one of them, does not light a lamp and sweep the house and seek diligently until she finds it? And when she has found it, she calls together her friends and neighbours, saying, 'Rejoice with me, for I have found the coin which I had lost.' Just so, I (Jesus) tell you, there is joy before the angels of God over one sinner who repents.

A drachma is worth the same as a denarius. Again we have the description of a scene from everyday life. The ten drachmas may represent enough to sustain life for two weeks. The money is hard earned, which is why the woman seeks it so intensively and celebrates with her neighbours when she finds it. And this fellowship of women, laughing in solidarity, becomes a parable of the joy of God, who rejoices not only by himself but with his angels. Those who have lost their way in life are called sinners. They no longer live with God but under the might of the powers of death. But it is possible to change one's life. God rejoices over that like this woman who has found the money she needs to survive on. The parable is

not meant to give an indirect picture of God but to open eyes to the fact that men and women experience God in their world, in their everyday life. In the eyes of the powerful men of antiquity a gossiping and laughing community of women was worthless; some of them would have called such women cackling hens. In Jesus' parable this group of women is made the place of God's revelation. The search, despair and joy of the woman is not just an image of something else, but indicates the seriousness with which God takes life.

A grain of mustard seed, Jesus relates in a parable, is the smallest seed on earth. Mustard was cultivated as a vegetable: some garden plants grew to a height of five feet and more. Look at the mustard seed that you sow—it turns into a marvellous plant. And now Jesus describes what a fantastic tree grows out of a tiny mustard seed: it has 'branches in which the birds of the air can nest' (Mark 4.32 par.). This conclusion to the short parable is a quotation from the Hebrew Bible (Dan. 4.9, 18; Ezek. 17.23; 31.6). The image of a mighty tree—often the cedar is mentioned—in whose branches the birds of the air nest is widespread in the Bible and in other Near Eastern texts. It is an image for a mighty empire in which many small peoples live as subjects in 'peace', a peace dictated by the powerful great king and conqueror. They are the birds which nest in the branches of the tree. God's kingdom—and in the introduction Jesus says that this is what it is about—can be recognized in the image of the sovereign cedar that grows from a grain of mustard seed. The dynamic of the parable is anarchical. It says that only God can be compared with the sovereign cedar. All the peoples in God's kingdom are on the same level as the birds in the branches. There are no longer conquerors and great kings. The anarchical dynamic can

50. Grinding flour. Tomb offering from ancient Egypt, *c.* 2000 BC.

also be recognized in the exciting assertion that God's rule over the world derives from a grain of mustard seed. Perhaps the story is meant to make people smile: a sovereign tree which is really a vegetable! In two of the three versions in which the parable has been handed down the word vegetable is used. A vegetable becomes the place of God's revelation, precisely because it is not the root of a cedar which is destined for great things. The parable directs attention to what is small and nourishing. God's kingdom is near, but it is not yet there. If you want to find his seed you must look at the very small grains.

This parable has often been interpreted in terms of the church: Jesus and his followers are the inconspicuous beginning of the mighty Christian church which issues in the kingdom of God. Such an interpretation in terms of the church misses Jesus' point. He did not want to give himself and his followers the status of a small founding community (even for a powerful church). Jesus—like his followers—was concerned to recognize where the 'last' are in society, the little ones, the superfluous who are imposed on by the successful.

Jesus did not engage in any political and social analysis along the lines of an ancient philosophy of the state or economy; however, he did consistently direct his attention to the little people and allied himself with them, whether these were the sick, prostitutes or children. Any grain of mustard seed can teach us to recognize the activity of God.

The parable of the mustard seed forms a pair with the parable of the leaven, even in the sources which are older than the written Gospels that we have: a man sows a mustard seed, a woman prepares dough: 'The kingdom of heaven is like leaven which a woman took and hid in three *sat* (= 39.4 litres) of meal, till it was all leavened' (Matt. 13.33 par.).

51. Egyptian baker, third century BC.

In the ancient world—as still in many poor countries which have not been completely industrialized—the bread-making is the daily work of women. Bread is the raw material of life, and bread-making is a basic necessity, work essential for life: one's own, and that of children and old people. It is creative work, and it is unpaid, often invisible, women's work, which is as unimportant for the plans of economic structures as giving birth. With this parable Jesus directs attention to a particular point of time in the preparation of dough, as if in a snapshot. The woman has mixed the flour with the yeast which makes it rise, covers the dough with flour and a cloth, and leaves it to stand in a warm place. Kneading such a great mass of dough is hard work. The poor find it painful. Now they can let their hands drop and wait until the dough has risen. It is at this moment, when a woman lets her hands drop and begins to wait, that the parable begins. Look at the hands of a woman who lets them drop after work. Here you see how God works and rests, how the kingdom of God is already there in dynamic and in rest. Soon its all-embracing power will transform the earth. It is not a matter of elaborating the details of the parable but of making God's nearness visible; God can be seen in everyday life, beside the bread trough. Jesus wants to open people's eyes to this. The work of women and men, work for life, is transparent to God's work and God's patience. From the perspective of a Western industrial society such an image may be too romantic—or it may sharpen people's gaze to what is work for human life and what is not—and what that has to do with God.

14

The Prodigal Son

The story of the prodigal son (Luke 15.11–32) is a love story which tells of seeking, losing and finding. Jesus clearly tells it as an answer to his critics who take offence at him: 'This man welcomes sinners and eats with them' (Luke 15.2). That is how Jesus' critics speak of him. Wrong converse with the wrong people is not seemly for a teacher of God; after all, he has to be able to distinguish between clean and unclean. The parable story with which Jesus answers this criticism arises out of the tension between an understanding of religion which marks out limits, which is orientated in ethical norms and rituals of everyday life and the festivals, and a prophetic understanding which, grounded in the Jewish tradition, hears the cry of the oppressed as the voice of God. What people take exception to in Jesus is his relationship to the poor, the outcast, the wretched. Because they were hungry, they did not observe the commandments about fasting but enjoyed themselves wherever they found something to eat. Jesus ate and drank with them, celebrated and discussed with them; they were and became his friends.

Jesus tells the parable of the father and the two sons in a culture of poverty in which the fate of impoverishment was a present threat at any time. The story itself takes place on a prosperous farm, which employed slaves and day labourers who enjoyed even less protection. As usual, the older son was

---

The best known parables in the New Testament include:

- The parable of the prodigal son (Luke 15.11–32)
- The parable of the workers in the vineyard (Matt. 20.1–16)
- The parable of the lost drachma (Luke 15.8–10)

- The parable of the mustard seed (Mark 4.30–32)
- The parable of the leaven (Matt. 13.33; Luke 13.20,21)
- The parable of the good Samaritan (Luke 10.25–37)

the heir to the farm, and as usual the younger son had his legacy paid out in advance as cash. For all the brothers due to inherit there was the hope that they could buy themselves some land somewhere and marry into a family. But not all younger sons succeeded in doing this, either because, as in the parable, they squandered their money and dealt carelessly with it, or because one of the constantly recurring famines drove up the price of corn and bread and in a flash the landless found themselves beggars.

So the departure of the younger son from home was usual in village life and was not a break with the family. It is perhaps unusual that the younger son himself claims his due. He has had no experience of dealing with money and for a short time leads a life of dissipation. The many poets who have spun out the story of the two sons and above all given it a dramatic setting have developed a colourful world of innkeepers, loose women, false friends and lusty songs, which stands in clear contrast to rural frugality dominated by doing one's duty and being obedient at work. In the end the money is all gone, and this experience, which is also unfamiliar to the young man, coincides with the kind of regional famine which often occurred in those days. The price of corn rises so high that even dry bread becomes too expensive (v. 14). He hires himself out as a swineherd and falls into the hands of an exploiter who even cheats him of the daily sustenance which is customary for herdsmen. He is not even allowed to touch

the pigs' food! The first dramatic turning point in the story is the desperate young man's decision to go home and at least be paid the wage of a day labourer there. He is

52. The Prodigal Son. Painting by Hieronymus Bosch (*c.* 1450–1516), Rotterdam, Boymans-van Beuningen Museum.

convinced that, unlike his older brother, he no longer has any right to live on the farm.

But the father does not behave like a testator, thinking in clearly legalistic terms. He has more maternal features. When he recognizes the starving man in rags as his son we are told that 'his heart contracted within him', he was in pain (v. 20). This aged Middle Eastern farmer then runs out to meet his son 'as fast as he could' (v. 20), contrary to all the rules of custom and respectability. This is a burlesque feature in the story which goes with the abundance of the man's happiness. The old father falls on the young man's neck before they exchange a word. He is simply happy to have his son home and kisses him in delight. He does not ask, as interpreters never tire of asking: 'What on earth have you been up to? How are you? What have you done with your substantial legacy?' Losing and finding again are the words which the father uses later (v. 32), and they stand for being dead and alive.

And life is staged as a festival with the fatted calf, with music, with new clothes, and, symbolized in the ring, with a new seal and new rights to the property, with singing and dancing. The joy and happiness of being together again have the first (v. 23) and the last (v. 32) word.

The interest of Jesus, the narrator, is not in making people small, helpless, broken. The prodigal son's confession is no condition; in this story the love is unconditional. It is what it is. The forgiveness given by the father in non-verbal form, in clothing and feasting, has no connection with the conditions of repentance, rending garments

53. The Return of the Prodigal Son. Painting by Leonello Spada (1576–1622), Paris, Musée du Louvre.

and confessing. It raises up the one who has been humiliated enough by life, and makes him new. The many abundances in the story of the prodigal son point to beauty, happiness, success, which in dogmatic terminology bear the name 'grace'.

What became of the older brother and how he can agree with his father and brother is not told in the story. This is probably one of the many questions which Jesus, who was also a marvellous teacher, left to the audience to answer. The father's behaviour towards his two sons also reflects Jesus' behaviour towards the people around him; it is a matter of seeking and lacking, meeting in both the literal and the metaphorical sense of the word. The father also comes to meet the older brother; he leaves the feast and invites the brother, who is standing outside, also to come in (v. 28). He asks him to 'make merry and be glad' (v. 32): joy, not sin, is the theme.

The theological statement of this story, which allows so many psychological interpretations, is the last one, in which the father says of his prodigal son: 'he was dead and is alive'. That separation from the father here means separation from the ground of life and not the resolution of an oedipal conflict points in advance to what 'resurrection' will mean in the Christian tradition. Remote from God, men and women are 'dead', incapable of joy. Jesus the narrator must have radiated something of the happiness of becoming free.

15

Eschatology: God is Near

In the Gospels, Jesus' message is often summed up in a few words: 'The time is fulfilled and the kingdom of God is at hand: repent and believe in the good news' (Mark 1.15; cf. Matt. 10.7 par.). 'Kingdom of God'—this central term takes its imagery from the royal palaces of the Near East and Rome. God rules like a great oriental king over the whole cosmos, over heaven and earth.

This idea, which is already ancient Jewish tradition, is politically provocative at root: only God is king, no one else. A political vision is bound up with the kingdom of God: all peoples have equal rights; only God is their ruler (see Mark 4.30–32 par., see p. 98 above). God's peace among the peoples is not based on subjection by a great king. The vision of equal rights for all peoples

54. Pantocrator. Ceiling mosaic, eleventh century, Daphne, Greece. In Byzantine art the divine ruler of the cosmos plays a central role— and reflects not least the claim to power of God's prime representative on earth, the Basileus.

is based on a deliberate contrast with the political present. The experiences of political rule are depicted in exclusively negative terms throughout the Jesus tradition: 'You know that those who are supposed to be rulers of the nations misuse their power, and their great men do violence to them' (Mark 10.42 par.).

After Jesus' death this political vision was impressively elaborated in the event of Pentecost. The peoples of the Mediterranean world spoke many languages and dialects, not just Greek, Latin and Aramaic. In the miracle of Pentecost everyone could suddenly understand the voice of God's messengers, although they were stammering, filled with the spirit ('speaking with tongues'); some of the onlookers interpreted this as drunken babbling. They heard these voices, each in his

or her own mother tongue (Acts 2.1–13). This is a vision which makes it clear that all people need their own culture, their own language, their own forms of religious expression. They are to hear Jesus' message of the nearness of God, but this is not to destroy their culture. This vision is clearly different from a world rule which prescribes both a single language and one state religion.

55. The Pentecost miracle. Book illustration from the Antiphonary of St Peter. Salzburg, late twelfth century.

Prayer
Everywhere I seek a city
with an angel before its gate.
I bear his great wing
broken off at the shoulder blade
and on the forehead his star as a
    seal.

And walk ever in the night ...
I have brought love into the
    world,
that each heart may blossom blue,
and have watched weary through
    a life,
in God veiled the dark breath.

Jesus proclaimed that God is near. He went around like a royal herald, even if his king was a king who did not use force and his messenger was the embodiment of 'meekness'. This was the opposite of the arrogance of power (Matt. 5.9; Luke 1.51f.). The nearness of God was the power which made possible the acts of justice and the words of healing which gave life. It was said that those who detected the nearness of God stood up and held their heads high (Luke 21.28). Many stories speak of rising, getting oneself up (for example Luke 13.10–17, see above). They are resurrection stories which show how the nearness of God changes people.

The kingdom of God is depicted with mythological images which derive from Jewish apocalyptic. We find Jewish 'apocalyptic' in many texts from this time. They are images of hope for people who have experienced that they no longer have anything to hope for in this life. They experience subjugation by foreign soldiers and see no end to it. But they hold firm to their God. Even if they do not experience any justice in their lifetime, even if they do not receive what is their due, they still evoke God as the incorruptible just judge. The sufferers complain to God, who hides his true face of justice, and hold fast to him in their grief. At the end of the day he will judge all humankind in accordance with the deeds of each individual. The perpetrators of injustice are delivered over to eternal death by God's final judgment. The just who have orientated themselves on God's will will be with God, take part in the banquet of the peoples in God's palace, and wear white garments. The will of God can be recognized by all. The Jews have it in the Torah and other people too know the basic commandments of God. They can know what justice is if they want to. These mythical images of judgment, of eternal death ('the outer darkness; there will be

O God, close your cloak firmly about me;
I know that I am in the glass globe of rest,
and even if the last human being forgets the world,
you do not again leave me out of omnipotence
and a new globe of earth closes around me.

Else Lasker-Schüler

wailing and gnashing of teeth', Matt. 22.13 etc.), and of eternal salvation at God's table have become incomprehensible to modern men and women. They sound cruel, and arouse the suspicion that this God judges in an arbitrary way, at his own

56. The opening of the fifth seal.
Painting by El Greco (1541–1614).
New York, Metropolitan Museum
of Art.

57. The fortress of Massada.   ▶

discretion. They also arouse the suspicion that they are nothing but vindictive fantasies of people who cannot defend themselves effectively. They need to be translated.

The decisive insight in more recent scholarship is that while these apocalyptic myths speak about the future, they refer to the present. They are meant to indicate the hour that has already struck: the hour has come for people to rise, even those who think that they are helpless. The helpless are to raise their heads. And the perpetrators of injustice are to know that they alone cannot determine what is right. They are to open their eyes and recognize the violence in which they are taking part. The nearness of God's future is a power that creates justice now, in the hour when men and women hear the word of the nearness of God.

In Western biblical scholarship since the end of the nineteenth century the idea has become established that Jesus expected the kingdom of God imminently. This meant that the end of world history was expected even in the generation of those alive at the time of Jesus. Not long after Jesus' death his followers would have understood that this imminent expectation was a mistake on Jesus' part. Now they settled down to live permanently in the world, for what came was not the kingdom of God but the church. This theory proved

highly persuasive to many people outside the scholarly world
as well. It is based on a linear view of time: God's future is
near and this nearness can be measured in days, months and
years, even if the specific length of time is unknown. World
history will end in the generation of those living now, in
God's great judgment. That is how Jesus' apocalyptic
mythology was understood.

Nowadays this theory has collapsed, because it has
become clear that the notion of time which it presupposes,
in the form of an infinite line into the future, was not that
of Jesus. Jesus and the Jewish people of his time do not
think in linear terms but in relationships, above all relationships to God. In their language there is not even a word
corresponding to the word 'future'. The next day is called
'what is to come' (*ta mellonta*, etc.). What is meant is God's
judgment, the resurrection, God's kingdom on this earth and
in heaven. The past, the story of this people, is a story of the
experiences of God's leadership, his goodness and his wrath.
'What is to come' is expected not only by suffering men and
women but also by God, with longing and hope. When, God,
will you fill heaven and earth? When at last will famine and
war cease?

The 'end' is longed for, but by it this apocalyptic does not
mean the end of history. It is the end of suffering on earth. So
apocalyptic, including Jesus' apocalyptic, is also rooted in the
present. Now is the hour of hope for God's kingdom. God is
near. The nearness of God cannot be measured in intervals of
time, but must be measured in the strength of the hope which
is spreading among people: 'The time is fulfilled and the
kingdom of God is at hand' (Mark 1.15). God's nearness has
consequences: 'Repent', change your 'disposition' (*metanoia*/
repentance literally means changing one's *nous*, mind, thought,

Telling the time
Our tree still bears no fruit
we still drive away the homeless
we do not allow the unemployed
   to work
we still hand over to the torturers
whatever they may need

and cut the throats of the poorest
so that their cry too does not
   disturb us

God still waits in vain
our time still lies in the hands of
   the mighty

At any rate he was executed
one of many the land was occupied
by the Roman emperor who had himself worshipped as God
a Jew like Jeshua was not worth much there
and this here made the people mad
with his stories and miracles
he healed people simply through love
and said it came from God

That was really nothing new
but now many people understood it afresh
how near God is and especially to those
who do not count in the game of the powerful
and some now walked more upright also the women
who sold themselves to bring up children
hope spread like a forest fire
hope for the new earth the kingdom of peace

Carola Moosbach

direction in life). You have reason to hope; resignation and the time of helplessness are coming to an end. The hopes that Jesus expresses bubble over, they are compelling: 'Blessed are your eyes, for they see, and your ears, for they hear. Truly, I say to you, many prophets and righteous men longed to see what you see, and did not see it ...' (Matt. 13.16f.). It is time to sing songs of praise. God has commissioned Jesus as his Messiah-liberator of the people to fill hearts with hope. Legend tells how already at his birth an old man (Luke 1.67–79) praised God because God's light could now be seen 'to lighten those who sit in darkness and in the shadow of death and to guide our feet into the way of peace.' God's goodness, which keeps calling creation into life, belongs with his dark side, his wrath. There is the time of jubilation, but also the time of growing and maturing. And there is the time

they pour poison into the rivers
amusement on to our screens
heavy metal into our food
and fear into our hearts

We still do not cry loudly enough
How long, God?

How long will you look on
without cutting down your fig
   tree?
We still have not learned to repent
we still rarely weep.

Still.

Dorothee Soelle

of terror at the end of security for those who will not hear and see although they could hear and see (for example Matt. 24.37–39). Thus the present is experienced as the time destined by God.

16

The Crucifixion

At the centre of the Christian religion stands the cross as the symbol for the death of Jesus. Nowhere is historical clarity about what we can know so important and so necessary as at this point in the life of Jesus, because here much of the reality of the death of Jesus has been suppressed and reinterpreted through dogmatic, anti-Jewish interests.

What we can know historically is that on a Friday in spring of a year between AD 26 and 36—the dates can only be estimates—Jesus of Nazareth was executed by Roman soldiers in Jerusalem. He was between thirty and thirty-five years old. Jesus was nailed by the hands and feet to a high wooden cross. Death by crucifixion is very slow and very painful. The lungs cannot function properly because the body is hanging. Those who are crucified slowly choke to death.

58. One of the most frequent motifs in art: the crucified Jesus. Modern Nigerian carving in wood.

Who was responsible for this death? Politically and legally it was the Roman governor Pontius Pilate. He was prefect of Judaea (his official title) from 26 to 36. In 1959 a Roman inscription bearing his name was found at Caesarea by the Sea (in present-day Israel). There is no such clear historical documentation for the life of Jesus of Nazareth, but the connection of his death with the name Pontius Pilate can be taken as historically reliable. The Christian confession of faith, the Apostles' Creed, the roots of which go back to this time, say that Jesus 'suffered under Pontius Pilate'. That is not meant to date the death of Jesus but to identify the author of the brutal execution. The legal circumstances are clear. In the Judaea of this time, as in many countries which in one way or other were under the rule of Rome, only the Roman governor had the right to pass death sentences and carry them out.

For what crimes were men and women condemned to crucifixion? Above all crimes with a political significance: desertion to the enemy, treachery, instigation to rebellion. In the case of Jesus the inscription on the cross gave as the reason for execution 'The king of the Jews' (Mark 15.26). From the perspective of Rome a man who was regarded as Messiah was a political danger. The Jewish historian Josephus reports about many Jewish movements in the time of Roman rule which gathered round a prophet, forerunner of God or Messiah. They expected the kingdom of God on earth and in heaven. As a rule they were unarmed. They developed ideas of a just and free society and therefore were regarded as a political danger by Rome. In this context the Roman inscription on Jesus' cross is part of the Roman policy towards Jewish religious liberation movements.

This thesis, that the crucifixion of Jesus was a misunderstanding of Jesus' activity as political action, fails to recognize

Crucifixion

The punishment of crucifixion was quite deliberately used by the representatives of Roman rule for the suppression of political unrest and danger. It was regarded as one of the most brutal ways of killing. In the lists of death penalties in Roman legal sources crucifixion appears at the end: it is regarded as worse than burning and condemnation to death by wild animals.

The Roman writer Apuleius tells in his romance *The Golden Ass* of a young girl from a good house who is captured by robbers in order to extort money from her parents. After her attempt to flee has failed,

the public effect of Jesus' expectation of the kingdom of God, which belongs in the history of Jewish resistance in the first century. It also belongs with the mass crucifixions reported by Josephus: 'The soldiers themselves through rage and bitterness nailed up their victims in various attitudes as a

59. The Ascent to Mount Calvary. Painting by Giovanni Battista Tiepolo, Venice, Sant'Alvise. The crowd accompanying the condemned man on the way to the place of execution makes the public character of the infliction of the punishment clear. On the right edge of the picture a man is carrying a tablet with the inscription INRI; the banner carried ahead bears the inscription SPQR, *Senatus populusque Romanorum*, 'the senate and the people of Rome', the authorities responsible for the execution.

the robbers devise a brutal death for her: 'The first thought that they should burn the maiden alive, the second that she should be thrown to the beasts, a third commanded that she should be nailed to the cross, but a fourth commanded that she should be tortured to death' (ch. 31,1). The robbers, like politicians and lawyers, agree that crucifixion is useful precisely because it is so cruel.

grim joke, till owing to the vast numbers there was no room for the crosses, and no crosses for the bodies' (Josephus, *Jewish War* 5).

What role did the people play at such killings? They were meant to be staged as publicly as possible. This public character of the executions, as far as possible like a popular festival, was in the interest of Roman rule over the then known world. Such a public death, whether slowly on the cross, or in the arena, where the condemned were torn apart by wild animals, was meant to be a deterrent, and indeed to find public approval.

The onlookers were to applaud the execution and thus state order. It is related that in the Gospels Pilate asked the crowd in front of his official residence in Jerusalem: '"What then do you want me to do with the one whom you call king of the Jews?" They cried ... "Crucify him!" Pilate said to them, "What evil has he done?" But they cried all the more, "Crucify him"' (Mark 15.12–14). The traditional interpretation of this scene exonerates Pilate and points to the crowd as

representative of the Jewish people, which is said to be guilty of the death of Jesus. This anti-Jewish interpretation has not reflected on Roman history. The crowd which shouts 'crucify him' is to be associated with Rome's bloody popular festivals. The crowd gathered in the arena is said to shout for the death of those condemned to the wild animals. There are seldom reports of the counter-voices which were also raised at such popular festivals.

The people about whom the Gospel of Mark reports in the rest of its narratives is always on Jesus' side. This Gospel is not concerned to incriminate the Jewish people but to identify the fear of men and women, whether they are disciples or other supporters from the people. The denial of Jesus by

◀ 60. The Colosseum in Rome, built AD 72–80. Here to entertain the people wild beasts were unleashed against men, and cruel gladiator fights and public executions took place.

61. Jesus before Pilate. Painting by Mihály von Munkácsy, c. 1881. Paris, Musée d'Orsay. Here the anti-Jewish interpretation by the artist is unmistakable.

Peter, his closest friend, stands for people's fear in the face of such a brutal threat. From the Roman perspective the men and women who followed those who were crucified were regarded as a political risk. A woman who wept publicly at the execution of her son was likewise nailed to the cross. Assent, jubilation, joy were the desired reactions. So the fear of the disciples, men and women, whom the Gospel of Mark in particular does not spare, is understandable. It was emphasized later to inculcate the bravery which the men and women who followed Jesus then showed despite their fear.

The descriptions of the crucifixion in the Gospels reflect this political reality. The mockery of the bystanders is a central element in the dramatic depiction of events—and a reaction which the Romans wanted. Jesus was mocked by passers

62. *Ecce homo* (Jesus and the Critics). Painting by James Ensor, 1891.

by, the chief priests and scribes, the Roman mercenaries (auxiliary troops) and the murderers who were crucified with him. They all agreed that there was a contradiction between what he did for others as a messianic prophet and what he did not do for himself: he healed others, he helped them, he gave them courage, but he himself was handed over mercilessly to the power of Rome. The mockery was politically desirable but at the same time there could be realistic reasons for it, and to the present day it has not fallen silent. Exactly what Jesus finally achieved is a question which cannot and may not be silenced in the face of hunger, impoverishment and ever-increasing violence. In Christian terms Jesus still hangs on the cross.

Are 'the' Jews to blame for the death of Jesus? For centuries Christianity has claimed that the Jews are murderers of God, that they are guilty of the crucifixion of Jesus. This assertion has justified pogroms against Jews. It is an important foundation on which Christian anti-Judaism and racist antisemitism have been built up. This deadly assertion has been backed up with statements from the New Testament about the involvement in the preparations for Pilate's sentence of crucifixion of men from the Jewish ruling classes like Caiaphas. This involvement will be historically correct. But it should not be misused to declare 'Judaism' guilty. Rather, we must ask about the various political interests among the Jewish leaders.

There were those who collaborated with Rome. The Herodian kings had different reasons for this collaboration from those of some high priests. The Herodian kings were minions of the rule of Rome, collaborators, as is shown by Herod's reported massacre of the children in Bethlehem. In the Gospel of John (11.48) a high priest is quoted who fears that as a

Blaise Pascal said: Jesus will be in agony until the end of the world; in this time one must not sleep. '*Jésus sera en agonie jusqu'à la fin du monde; il ne faut par dormir en ce temps-là.*'

Heinrich Boll remarked: 'Good Friday—now it is time to console God.'

result of his success among the Jewish people Jesus could seem to the Romans to be a political threat: this is a very realistic estimation of the situation. The people's guilt in the death of Jesus is a later interpretation that arose once the earliest Christian community had separated from Judaism. Conversely, after the Shoah we must recognize the guilt that Christianity has brought upon itself through this assertion. It is an abiding legacy which must be worked through, by future Christian generations as well.

If we want to know how Jesus died in a spiritual sense of the word the best evidence is given by the 'seven last words' which have been handed down in the New Testament tradition. They cannot be proved historically; none of those who handed them down was present when Jesus whispered them or cried them out, but they show how his death was understood within the fellowship of rising Christianity. It is possible that Jesus died with a loud cry. But what is probably the earliest tradition puts the beginning of Psalm 22 on his lips: 'My God, my God, why have you forsaken me?' (Mark 15.34). Tradition has it that the church father Augustine did not believe that Christ cried this out, because of his divine nature. But the tradition of the psalms leaves room for complaint, indeed despair, at the one who promised help and life; in the 'Why?' we can also hear Jesus holding fast to the God who has promised life. The Jesus who speaks here is a son of God who has become like us—to the depths of god-forsakenness. Therefore he holds firm to the complaint, and that means to the one whom he accuses.

Luke has maintained many conciliatory features which tone down the solitude of the dying man. He has Jesus pray for his torturers, 'Father, forgive them, for they know not what they do' (Luke 23.34). This is said about the soldiers, the

The dramatic **Jewish resistance** against Rome has left many archaeological traces on Jewish soil. In 1969, during the excavation of a rock tomb, the heel bones of a crucified man by the name of Yohanan were found. The nail could no longer be removed from the bone, otherwise it would have been used for further crucifixions. The political resistance of the oppressed had a last effective means of expression: their own bodies.

slaves of war, who have to do what they are told. It is a saying which gives love of enemy a face, even if the soldiers then throw dice for the garments of the tortured man. The other sentence that Luke hands down is also a conciliatory saying, spoken to one of the murderers crucified with Jesus, who asks Jesus to think of him when he enters his kingdom. 'Today,' Jesus tells him, 'you will be with me in paradise' (Luke 23. 43). Here Jesus plays a king, one who hangs on the gallows and promises life to another who is hanging on the gallows: life, freedom and a good outcome. Perhaps this crazy language of hope can be spoken only when there is nothing left to back it up. The love and the pain say not only what is true but also what is needed. The love and the pain reach

The Word
None of his words
I believed, he would not have
cried: God, why
have you forsaken me?

That is my word, the word
of the lowest human being.

And because he himself
was so far below, a
man who cries 'why?' and
cries 'forsaken', therefore
one could also believe
the other words,
those from further up,
perhaps
believe him.

Rudolf Otto Wiemer

with their language into the land where tears are wiped away. It is the victims who do not cease to sing the song of the good outcome of things—and they are the only ones from whom one can believe this language.

The extraordinary effect of Jesus' message throughout

63. James Dean and Elizabeth Taylor in *Giant*, 1955. The resemblance to depictions of the crucifixion is unmistakable.

history is connected with his passion in the double sense of this word. This 'passion' is the story of the suffering of someone who was tortured to death and at the same time the passion of a crazy man who could not give up love of life in its fullness for all. Here in Luke's 'Into your hands I commend my spirit' (Luke 23.46) are his last words.

John's tradition makes Jesus die with the words 'It is fulfilled' (John 19.30). Shortly beforehand, the tormented man says, 'I thirst', a motif of the torment in this kind of torture, which in the other reports emerges without a word, visible and tangible only for those standing by. The fulfilment here also includes care of those left behind, shown in an exemplary way in the persons of Jesus' mother and the beloved disciple John. The woman under the cross inherits a son and the son inherits a mother. The dying man has no more to give. Jesus leaves people to one another; none need warm himself or herself, none need provide for himself or herself. Each mothers the other, each is comforted. The Jesus who dealt like this with his followers is also the Jesus who enables people to see 'Christ' dwelling in other people, in the eyes of the street children in Bogota or the forsaken drinkers in our cities.

Embracing the cross is a Christian gesture which chooses life. It means taking into account the difficulties, the lack of

For the revolutionary Jesus on his birthday

It is almost two thousand years
since you left the world,
the sacrificial lamb of life!
You gave the poor their God.
You were mocked by the rich.
You did it in vain!
You saw violence and police.
You wanted all people free
and peace on earth.
You knew how that causes misery
and wanted all people good,
so that it became more beautiful!
You were a revolutionary
and made life hard for yourself
with black marketeers and
   scholars.
You always protected freedom

and exploited no one.
You came to the wrong people!
You fought bravely against them
and against state and industry
and the whole mob.
Until because nothing worked
they committed judicial murder
   on you.
It was just like today.
People were not ready.
At least Christianity
for all its folded hands.
You loved them in vain.
You died in vain. And everything
   remained
as it was.

Erich Kästner

success, the fear of standing alone. This tradition has never promised us a garden of roses. Embracing the cross today means growing up into resistance. And the cross will grow green and blossom. We love the cross to excess. We grow in suffering. We are the tree of life.

This understanding of the cross also leads us into a deep understanding of talk about resurrection, which many people often find strange. People have greater problems with the resurrection than with almost any other statement of faith.

And yet people begin to experience resurrection when, both then and now, they are ready for crucifixion. There are two reasons for this. The first reason is the cross, which cannot be separated from the resurrection if one wants to retain what it all means. Belief in the resurrection roots us in the old story and in our own. The festival of Easter does not celebrate the exodus into post-history which has now at last been attained, something that comes after historical suffering; it celebrates history itself, this emergence from un-freedom. Without the primal story from the Hebrew Bible about the exodus of the children of Israel from the house of slavery in Egypt, one cannot also understand the exodus of Jesus from the house of the dead.

The other reason is our own life, which we do not want to separate from the death and life of Jesus, nor separate even from the defeat and victory of the life of God. Easter is either

64. Crucifixion. Photography by Bettina Rheims, 1998.

existential, or it says nothing at all and is rightly exploited commercially.

Whether a pseudo-death, a revival and the breaking of the laws of nature are a sure foundation for what happened in Palestine two thousand years ago we do not know. It is certain that this kind of discussion diverts us skilfully from something else, namely the judicial murder which was committed against the poor devil from Nazareth. What we know objectively is that like many before him and after him he was slowly and cruelly tortured to death. He could have avoided that by flight, by withdrawing into the private sphere, by transcendental meditation or other escapades which lead away from reality. Instead of that he remained loyal to his cause; love of those who had been robbed of rights and possessions, 'the last', as he liked to call them. For these last, for those who were regarded as the dregs, he developed a new way of living with friends, men and women. He did not want to be better off than the poorest. Therefore he lived without violence and without protection against violence.

17

Died for our Sins: The Atoning Death

An interpretation of the history of Israel runs through the Hebrew Bible and the post-biblical Jewish tradition which is central to understanding the Christian teaching about the death of Jesus. When the temple is destroyed and the people can no longer live with its God, but are deported and maltreated, this is an expression of their common guilt before God. Otherwise the enemy would have no power over them.

65. *Paso* (procession group): erection of the cross. A group of painted wood sculptures by Francisco Rincón, 1604. Valladolid, Museo Nacional de Escultura.

Here is an example from the Hebrew Bible: 'O Lord, why do you make us err from your ways and harden our heart, so that we do not fear you? Return for the sake of your servants, the tribes of your heritage. Your holy people possessed your sanctuary a little while; our adversaries have trodden it down. We have become like those over whom you have never ruled, like those who are not called by your name' (Isa. 63.17–19). In the first century AD the economic and spiritual existence of the people was threatened. People interpreted their fear of what was still to come with the help of the biblical tradition, which was based on historical experiences. Will God go away again, and will their Roman enemies lead the people into exile, to become prisoners of war and to be raped? The death of martyrs who opposed the violence of Rome became a sign of hope. The power of the enemy over the people could be interrupted.

There is a Jewish theology of martyrdom which for political reasons constantly understands the suffering under Babylonians, Persians or Romans as the guilt of the subject people itself.

This background also governs the interpretation of the crucifixion of Jesus in the New Testament. It plays a part in the history of the suffering and resistance of the Jewish people. The New Testament assimilation of Jesus' death on the cross in ritual and theological reflections belongs within the history of the theology of Jewish martyrdom. Jesus' death was interpreted as death for the sin of the people—'for our sins'—or also as an atoning sacrifice and ransom for the captive people. There is a Jewish Hellenistic text from this period (between Pompey and Vespasian) which is helpful for understanding the New Testament interpretation of the death of Jesus as liberation of the people from sin in the face of God.

Every time has its sin, God.
Our sin is resignation.
We have hope only on our lips,
our hearts are empty.

Every time has its sin, God.
Our sin is short-windedness.

We do not want to understand
that the fight for our children and
    grandchildren,
with our children and
    grandchildren, goes on.
The air has gone out of us,
we can no longer breathe easily.

There we read about martyrs: 'These then, having consecrated themselves for the sake of God, are now honoured not only with this distinction but also by the fact that through them our enemies did not prevail against our nation, and the tyrant was punished and our land purified, since they became, as it were, a ransom for the sin of our nation. Through the blood of these righteous ones and through the propitiation of their death the divine providence rescued Israel, which had been shamefully treated' (IV Macc. 17.20ff.). Through their death the martyrs purify and sanctify the soul of the people, which has been stained by sin. Here old ideas about sacrifice, according to which the blood of sacrificial animals brings about the purification of the people, are used in a secondary way and reality is interpreted with their help: thus God is again united with his people, and the enemies no longer have power over the people, for it has not remained silent. The tradition in the Christian liturgies of saying a general confession of sin has also lost none of its liberating power in the present. The community becomes the place of clarity and analysis, of lament and at the same time of liberation.

After Jesus' death, first the women and then also the men who had worked with Jesus understood that this death was not the end of their hopes for the liberation of Israel, but had brought liberation. The people was free from captivity, free from guilt, free from the power of the oppressor, united with its God. There is a new beginning wherever people believe in this liberation and realize it in their lives. The Christian eucharist was the effective rite which emerged from the Jewish theology of martyrdom and shaped the remembrance of Jesus in Christianity. The remembrance of the death of the martyr became the centre of a shared solemn supper and the source of the hope that the power of God is greater than the power of death.

Every time has its sin, God.
Our sin is fear.
We submit to the pressure that
    comes from above.
Independence, self-confidence and
    trust in God
have departed from us.

On the cross of Christ
your lack of courage became faith,
your loneliness love,
your resignation hope.

Luise Schottroff

In the post-Christian world the Christian term 'sin' has been devalued and is now used mainly for self-indulgence, traffic offences or sexual misbehaviour. A serious understanding of sin denotes separation from God as separation from God's will, namely life in its fullness for all the inhabitants of earth. People can separate themselves from God by specific actions—like theft, rape or murder—but also by a wrong way of living and failing to act where intervention rather than looking away is called for (cf. the story of the Good Samaritan, Luke 10.29–37). This understanding of sin, which is committed by looking away, acting in ignorance and not taking an active part, is indispensable for a theology after Auschwitz and similarly determines the way in which liberation theology and feminism think about this basic concept. What separates me from God, what separates me from life in its fullness? That is a different form of knowledge which is needed today for understanding Jesus' teaching.

Holy Saturday 81

And when finally
the graves are empty
and the exhumation of the
murdered is in vain
and the photos disappear
of children sprayed with a new
     poison
which makes their skin black and
     peel off
and the eyes sunken
and when finally
the graves are empty
of mutilated corpses
in El Salvador

When I began to become a
     Christian
I wanted to see Christ
striking me on the way to
     Damascus
I imagined this place like
     Göttingen
the empty tomb was only a fairy
     story
for unenlightened people

Now I've already been too long
becoming a Christian
and probably have seen
Jesus occasionally
most recently as an old woman in
     Nicaragua
who is learning to read and she
     shone
not only her eyes but also
her thinning hair
and the crippled feet
she simply shone

But I have also become poorer
and go depressed through the city
also go to demonstrate as if
     courage were distributed there
and would love to see for my life
the other half of the story,
the empty tomb of Easter morning
and the empty tombs in El
     Salvador

                    Dorothee Soelle

18

Resurrection

The Roman historian Tacitus, an enemy of developing Christianity, wrote about Christ that after his execution by Pontius Pilate his following increased unexpectedly and rapidly: 'The deadly superstition (i.e. Christianity), thus checked for the moment, again broke out not only in Judaea, the first source of the evil, but also in Rome, where all things hideous and shameful from every part of the world meet and become popular' (*Annals* 15.44). That was an outsider's view of the event which the followers of Jesus called his resurrection. The representatives of the world power, Rome, took the resurrection of martyrs into their political calculations, as the following scene shows. Herod Antipas, who had had John the Baptist executed, hears with concern that it is said among the people that Jesus is the Baptist risen again. He even believes it himself. 'The people

66. Publius Cornelius Tacitus, Roman historian (*c.* AD 55–120). Engraving by Fritzsche, 1764, coloured later.

said: John the Baptizer has been raised from the dead; that is why these powers are at work in him' (Mark 6.14-16). In the eyes of the people, and also in the king's eyes, the mighty acts of Jesus, his healings of the sick, his message of liberation by God, continue the work of John the Baptist. It was said among the people that the messianic prophet ('the Egyptian') had not been executed but 'disappeared' (see above pp. 19ff.). From their perspective that meant that he would come again, or someone else would continue his work. So those who executed the messianic prophets could not lean back content; the rebellion, the unrest among the people would go on, for his executed prophets were restless dead. Resurrection faith has its context among the people 'who sit in darkness' (Luke 1.79) and hunger to be able to live before their God 'in holiness and righteousness' (Luke 1.75).

Belief in the resurrection of the crucified Messiah Jesus takes a unique and special form, and without this belief Christianity would not have come into being. In Judaism the expectation of the coming of God as king over earth and heaven was bound up with the expectation of the resurrection of the dead. God will judge humankind, those still alive and those already dead, and afterwards the righteous will rise to life. Sometimes this resurrection was further elaborated on: all the bones would be collected together again and would be given back their flesh. There were old prophecies which foretold the resurrection of the humiliated people: 'Thus says God,

68. Resurrection of Jesus as the redemption of Adam and Eve—representing all human kind—from death. Greek icon, *c.* 1600.

Adonai, to these bones: See, I will cause breath to enter you, and you shall live. And I will lay sinews upon you, and will cause flesh to come upon you, and cover you with skin, and put breath in you, and you shall live' (Ezek. 37.5f.). The bodies of the dead are not forgotten by God and they remain in the collective memory of the people of God. In the Jewish tradition the memory of history and the dead is part of faith, part of Jewish identity.

This tradition has also lasted down the centuries in some areas of Christianity, for example in the custom of burying the dead in the earth and not cremating them, because in this

69. The other interpretation of the resurrection: Jesus triumphant. Painting by Matthias Grünewald, 1513–15. Isenheim Altar, Colmar, Unterlinden Museum.

◄ 67. Christ mourned. A terra-cotta group by Niccolò dell'Arca, 1462–63. Bologna, Pinacoteca Nazionale.

way their bodies will be preserved for the resurrection. The dead belong to the living. The expectation of the resurrection of the dead starts from the fellowship experienced between the living and the dead, and it takes human bodies quite seriously. God has created the bodies, and he will give the dead new bodies. By contrast, the dualistic belief in the immortality of the individual soul which is frequently to be found in present-day Christianity has no biblical roots and regards the human body as incidental.

The resurrection of the dead to eternal life is an expression of the hope that injustice will not prove victorious. This hope says that even if the violence of human beings against one another wins a definitive victory in murder, this victory is only apparently definitive.

Thus in early Christianity Jesus' resurrection was not interpreted as a unique event, as it still is in later Christian dogma. It was important for the people who believed in Jesus that all the dead should rise. They said: 'He is the firstfruits of those who have fallen asleep' (I Cor. 15.20 etc.).

Time and again it has been said by critics of the resurrection faith that all human beings decompose, and Jesus decomposed too. That is a criticism of church dogma, which requires Christians to believe in the breaking of the laws of nature and the unique miracle of the resurrection of Jesus. But whether Jesus' tomb was empty after his resurrection or whether one could have photographed the risen Christ are not questions which troubled the people who learned to believe in the resurrection of Jesus.

The Gospels tell many stories about friends and above all women friends of Jesus who went to his tomb in search of the living Christ.

70. Checking the women's ▶
report: Peter and John hasten to the tomb on the morning of the resurrection. Painting by Eugène Burnand, 1898. Paris, Musée d'Orsay.

But on the first day of the week, at early dawn, they went to the tomb, taking the spices which they had prepared. And they found the stone rolled away from the tomb, but when they went in they did not find the body.

While they were perplexed about this, behold, two men stood by them in dazzling apparel; and as they were frightened and bowed their faces to the ground, the men said to them,

'Why do you seek the living among the dead? Remember how he told you, while he was still in Galilee, that the Son of man must be delivered into the hands of sinful men, and be crucified, and on the third day rise.'

And they remembered his words. And returning from the tomb they told all this to the eleven and all the rest (Luke 24.1–9).

The women at the tomb did not have the problems of the European Enlightenment and its criticism of the church. They looked into the tomb because they were sad, indeed desperate, that their hope for the liberation of Israel had once again come to an end through military force. That they found the

tomb empty without Jesus in it still meant nothing to them. Indeed they were even criticized by the two angels who met them at the tomb: 'Why do you seek the living among the dead?' They should have remembered that Jesus predicted his death and his resurrection and they should have drawn conclusions from this memory long ago. Their task is to proclaim his resurrection and carry on his actions. 'Jesus lives, I live with him', is a summary of the resurrection story in a hymn. 'Death, where now are your terrors?' continues the writer, Christian Fürchtegott Gellert (1752). Here 'death' is the death of Jesus as the end of the story of the man from Nazareth and at the same time death as the end of hope, as the quenching of the vision of another life which people could live with one another. It is a death which is omnipresent today wherever people are reduced, and allow themselves to be reduced, to our existing culture with its Western stamp.

At the end of the Gospel of Luke we are told quite emphatically how the risen Christ has time and again to appear to his disciples so that they finally understand that they are not to despair, but have to carry on the work for the liberation of Israel. Really they do not need any appearances of the dead, nor any empty tomb or heavenly messenger. The memory of Jesus' words and his way of living tells them what is to be done now; it frees them from anxiety and paralysing despair. The final chapter of Luke tells the story of the two disciples making their way to Emmaus. It is a way of hopeless sorrow. 'But we hoped that he would redeem Israel' (Luke 24. 21). The answer of the traveller who goes with them, whom they do not recognize as Jesus, refers to Moses and all the prophets; it is a reference to the power of the tradition which supports them and will also support them now. 'Did not our hearts burn within us when he spoke with us on the way,

The learned theologian **Christian Fürchtegott Gellert** (1715–69) was highly esteemed by his contemporaries for his writings, which were influenced by Enlightenment ideals. He composed stage works (comedies and melodramas), novels and a great many poems which expressed his devout pietism. The 'Spiritual Odes and Songs' (1757), which were also set to music by some of the composers of his time, were very much to eighteenth-century taste. From 1751 Gellert worked in Leipzig as Professor of Poetry and Rhetoric.

when he opened the scriptures to us?' (Luke 24.31), they ask later, when they have recognized the man travelling with them and he has disappeared again. The other help that Jesus gives them is the bread shared with them; it is the remembrance of the shared meal in which he was and will be present. Scripture and sacrament are what remains, even if Jesus has disappeared from sight.

So the answer to the present-day question whether the tomb was empty or full should be this. Jesus' followers certainly thought that the body of Jesus was no longer in the tomb, but this view was not yet belief in the resurrection. Belief in the resurrection is also independent of ideas about biology. For present-day awareness, stamped by the natural

71. Landscape with Christ on the road to Emmaus. Painting by Claude Lorrain, 1660. St Petersburg, Hermitage Museum.

Song on the Road to Emmaus
We've already gone a long way
from the city of our hope
to a village where things are said to be better

> Didn't we believe
> we could overcome fear
> the fear of the old piece-worker
> of being declared sick
> the fear of the Turkish girl
> of being deported
> the fear of the tormented neurotic
> of being shut up
> for ever

We've already gone a long way
in the same wrong direction
away from the city of our hope
to the village where there is said to be water

> Didn't we think
> we were free and could liberate
> all the ruined types
> the child worker falling behind and being punished
> the boy on his moped
> sent to the wrong work
> a whole lifetime
> the man who is deaf and dumb
> in the wrong country
> at the wrong time
> made dumb by work
> for bread alone
> a whole lifetime

We went so far
in the same wrong direction
away from the city of our hope
which still lies buried there

> Then we met someone
> who shared his bread with us
> who showed the new water
> here in the city of our hope

> I am the water
> you are the water
> he is the water
> she is the water

sciences, an empty tomb is in any case the result of grave robbery. But even if people today can only imagine that like the bodies of all men and women the body of Jesus decomposed in the tomb, belief in the resurrection is still a force in life independent of tombs, whether empty or full. Resurrection faith perhaps makes different images for itself from those it made then, but the continuation of the actions of Jesus and the longing for the other, eternal, life still constitutes Christian identity. 'Eternal' does not mean an endless prolongation of life for individuals, but accords with the creation which God called 'good', which includes coming and going. Both the dead and those born later have a place in it. They are inscribed in God's book and God reads their names. 'I believe in

72. Resurrection of Christ. Painting by El Greco, 1605–10. Madrid, Museo del Prado.

Then we turned round and went
into the city of buried hope
back to Jerusalem

    The one with water is going with us
    the one with bread is going with us
    we will find the water
    we will be the water
    I am the water of life
    you are the water of life
    we are the water of life
    you are the water of life
    we will be the water

Dorothee Soelle

eternal life', says the Christian creed. A sentence which can often be read in death notices contents itself with 'No one is dead until the last person who recalls him or her is dead.' It is a sentence which denies the God who remembers and has inscribed everyone in the book of life. When we speak of eternal life we spell out what the Jewish tradition expresses by the sentence 'God is memory'.

Today we are looking for a language which can name this mystery of the world which the friends of Jesus experienced as resurrection. The Jesus movement found a traditional language for that after Jesus' death in new, quite distinctive forms of expression. The celebration of the resurrection early on Sunday morning and the remembrance of the last supper held firm to the indestructible hope of life for all creation.

On resurrection
They ask me about the resurrection
I've certainly heard of it
that a person no longer hastens towards death
that death can be behind one
because love is before one
that fear can be behind one
the fear of being abandoned
because I myself have heard of it
certainly there is nothing there
it could go on for ever

Oh, do not ask me about the resurrection
a fairy tale from age-old times
which one quickly forgets
I listen to those
who dry me out and belittle me
I turn towards
becoming slowly accustomed to being dead
in the heated dwelling
the great stone before the door

Oh, do not ask me about resurrection
oh, do not stop asking me

Dorothee Soelle

Postscript

Today many people in the rich world think that Jesus of Nazareth is a figure of history who belongs in a museum but not in the reality of contemporary life. But even in the post-Christian context people still detect time and again how Jesus comes out of the museum of history and is a challenge and a consolation for human life. On the other hand, belief in Jesus is most endangered by those who are anxious to preserve it. They are afraid of changes to established customs of thinking and living; they see reforms as destructive and would much prefer to hide Jesus in a golden shrine—untouchable and therefore also touching no one, unchangeable and therefore never changing anyone, eternally valid and therefore as far removed as possible from our reality.

73. Inca Madonna. Painting, *c.* 1680.

But God did not become human in order, to speak metaphorically, to remain in his heaven or his museum, and the changes of faith belong in the history of the incarnation of God. Incarnation means that faith has a history, an incomplete history with an open horizon which sets our possibilities free.

Now this open horizon relates not only to the questions which formerly were resolved with the help of 'dogma' or 'liturgy'; it is even more applicable to practical questions of Christian lifestyle. The Christian ethic is open-ended. What will it look like in the future? What attitude will be a model for it? What individual and social virtues will it comprise? What can we learn from Christ for our present and our future?

Here we use the word 'Christ' because it cannot be enough to look to the historical Jesus for such learning, the value of which is not historical but practical. Those who have learned from Jesus' life and words will not be content with remaining there and ignoring his ongoing history. For two thousand years this Jesus of Nazareth has been risen. He changes the consciousness of people who believe in his promise. Since him and in him hope for the world has grown, and there is more reason to have courage. In his name the face of the world has been changed. When we speak of Christ we take what Francis of

74. Madonna with child. Wood statuette from the Solomon Islands.

Assisi or Martin Luther King learned of Jesus into our relationship; we take over the treasures which people have gathered in their encounters with Jesus. He is the Christ who is understood, who has been developed in specific ways, the Christ who goes before us and continues to be active, from whom we can learn. This way from Christ to us has not been in vain.

But if we are to recognize it as the way of Christ, we must reflect on the man from Nazareth, because history also sees the appearance of the misunderstood, the propped-up Christ, who is made to serve people's own interests, who can so easily be manipulated. Those who simply go on talking about him in the words of the fathers manipulate him because with the words of the fathers they are at the same time attempting to preserve the world of the fathers and are thus keeping the present world distant from this Christ, whether they want to or not. It is always only the Christ who becomes present and who speaks the truth to us about our life in our present reality who is risen. The one from whom we learn nothing, who does not change us and who does nothing to make our conscience more sensitive, remains dead.

75. A votive medallion of the kind that can often be found in Spain and Latin-American countries, for example in taxis and on household altars.

Glossary
by Beate Wehn and John Bowden

*The glossary contains brief explana-
tions of biblical terms and the technical
theological vocabulary used in the book.
Bibliographical references at the end of
the explanations are to titles mentioned
in the Bibliography, which reflect the
current theological discussion on the
particular theme and are worth
consulting.*

Androcentrism: from the Greek
aner, andros = the male; male-
centredness denotes a structure of privilege which regards the life and experiences
of adult males as universal.
Today it is necessary to
understand that the androcentric perspective is not
objective and needs to be
relativized. The Bible is
written in androcentric language, but it can be deci-
phered with historical means
so that parts of the history of
women and children become
visible.
See Schottroff, *Lydia's Impatient Sisters*; Schüssler-
Fiorenza, *In Memory of Her*

Anti-Judaism: hostility to Jews and
a devaluation of Judaism on a
theological basis, which stems
above all from Christianity.
Anti-Jewish theological arguments claim that the two religions are essentially opposed
and that Judaism has been
'superseded' by Christianity.
By contrast the anti-Judaism

debate which has been carried
on in Germany especially
since the 1970s has developed
out of the insight that Christian anti-Judaism made a
central contribution towards
the rise of racist antisemitism.
See Farmer, *Anti-Judaism and
the Gospels*; Rubenstein and
Roth, *Approaches to Auschwitz*

Apocalyptic: a genre of literature
which claims to 'unveil'
things which are normally
hidden. In Jewish tradition
around the time of Jesus this
was an oppressed people's
vision of hope for the future,
often expressed in bizarre
imagery.
See Theissen and Merz, *The
Historical Jesus*; Rowland,
Christian Origins

Census: In AD 6 Judaea was put
under Roman administration.
Usually there was a census in
connection with the establish-
ment of Roman provinces,
i.e. lists were made for the
future taxation of the population, by both land tax
(*tributum soli*) and poll tax
(*tributum capitis*) payable to
Rome. Brutal interrogations
were a matter of course in
such censuses and often there
were revolts.
See Wengst, *Pax Romana*

Cleanness/uncleanness, cultic: In
the Bible cleanness and uncleanness have nothing to do

with cleanliness and dirt. What is meant, rather, is cultic, ritual cleanness as corresponding to God's holiness. The question underlying the regulations about cleanness is: how can human beings encounter the powerful presence of God? Ideas and regulations about cleanness have a specific reference to the temple cult and to the conscious hallowing of everyday life. Cultic uncleanness—for example as a result of contact with corpses and dead animals or the emission of male or female bodily fluids—was a temporary state which could be ended by rituals of purification. If a person was in a state of cultic uncleanness, he or she was not segregated socially in everyday life but was merely not in a position to take part in cultic actions, for example in the temple. Cleanness and uncleanness were a subordinate matter in synagogue worship.
See Countryman, *Dirt, Greed and Sex*; Sanders, *Judaism*

Dogma: the official statement of a faith community which is binding on its members.
See Soelle, *Thinking about God*

Eschatology: the doctrine of the last things. In the time of Jesus this took the form of an expectation of divine intervention in the course of human history to destroy oppressive powers and to bring justice to God's people. Jesus' preaching took this up, but saw God's intervention primarily in favour of the outcast and oppressed.
See Theissen and Merz, *The*

Historical Jesus; Rowland, *Christian Origins*

Gentile Christianity: The term conceals an anti-Judaistic notion which is concerned at a very early stage to construct a 'church of the nations' and to depict this as being as independent as possible of Jewish roots ('free of the law'). In this interpretation people from the nations who came to be followers of Christ did not adopt Jewish practices but rejected them. The historical reality looks different: for people from the nations, up to the middle of the second century discipleship of Christ as a rule meant entry into Jewish-Christian communities and the adoption of Jewish practices.
See Schottroff, *Lydia's Impatient Sisters*

Halakhah: Derived from the Hebrew verb (*halakh*: go, walk, behave), *halakhah* denotes establishing the way that Israel is to go to God. This way is discussed on the basis of the Torah and related to the particular demands of the present. Thus *halakhah* is a never-ending process.
See Musaph-Andriesse, *From Torah to Kabbalah*

Hebrew Bible: Christian theologians reflecting on the problem of anti-Judaism use the designation Hebrew Bible as an alternative to the traditional term Old Testament. The designation Old Testament was introduced by the early church in the process of separation from Judaism. But it is increasingly felt to be a problem: in legalistic thought a new testament invalidates an old one. And in fact this understanding coincides with the anti-Jewish claim that the so-called New Testament has superseded or replaced the Old Testament.

The designation Hebrew Bible is an attempt to counter anti-Judaism even at the level of language. Jews also speak of the Hebrew Bible, which contains the Pentateuch (i. e. the five books of Moses), the prophetic books and the writings.

Law/Torah: In English translations of the Bible the Hebrew word *torah* is usually translated 'law'. This is encouraged by the Greek translation of *torah* with *nomos* = law. In the Jewish tradition *torah* means God's instructions for life and teaching for the well-being of the people of Israel. Expressed in the language of Christian dogmatics, the Torah comprises both 'law' and 'gospel'. In Judaism it is highly esteemed as the basis of life and faith and as a gift, a benefit bestowed by God over which people rejoice and which they celebrate in a relaxed way (cf. Pss. 1; 19; 119). Where 'law' appears in biblical translations—and also in the New Testament—the Torah of Israel should therefore be thought of as 'instruction'.
See Crüsemann, *The Torah;* Sanders, *Judaism*

Logia source (Q): Literary criticism of the New Testament starts from the so-called two-source theory, which recognizes the Gospel of Mark as the oldest

Gospel: it served as a basis for the Gospels of Matthew and Luke. In addition Matthew and Luke also use parallel material which does not come from Mark. For these texts a separate source is assumed which can only be reconstructed in parts; it is called the Logia source (Q, from the German for source, *Quelle*). So Matthew and Luke make use of traditions from Mark and the Logia source. In addition there are texts peculiar to Matthew or Luke. These are called the special material of Matthew or Luke.
See Theissen and Merz, *The Historical Jesus*

Martyr: one who has been persecuted, maltreated and executed for his or her faith. Martyrs did not withstand their many torments out of a delight in suffering and masochism, but saw the endurance of martyrdom as the only possible way of offering resistance to the caprice, violence and cruelty of imperial rule.
See Theissen and Merz, *The Historical Jesus*

Messiah: comes from the Hebrew *mashah* = 'anoint' and means 'anointed'. The Greek translation is *christos*. Having been anointed, the kings of Israel were initially understood as rulers appointed by God. In time another view arose: the expectation that one day there would be a historical liberator from the house of David who would put an end to all foreign rule and redeem the people Israel. The quite different Jewish messianic hopes are inseparably connected

with concrete social, political and economic revolutions on earth and the hope of justice and peace.
See Theissen and Merz, *The Historical Jesus*

Messian: here used as a designation for the Jesus movement and for the people who after Jesus' death regarded him as the expected Messiah.

Messianic movements: In the first century, alongside the Jesus movement there was a variety of messianic movements, each of which saw its leader as the longed-for Messiah. One of the best-known instigators of such a movement is Bar-Kochba, who ventured on a new and ultimately unsuccessful revolt against Rome in AD 132–135.
See Schottroff, *Lydia's Impatient Sisters;* Theissen and Merz, *The Historical Jesus*

New Testament: The New Testament is a collection of writings originally in Greek, most of which come from the first century (thus the authentic letters of Paul, the Gospels, Acts of the Apostles and most of the short letters). Other texts (like the Pastoral Epistles, Jude and II Peter) possibly come from the time when the separation of Christianity from Judaism was already well advanced. Most writings of the New Testament are to be read and interpreted as Jewish writings building on the tradition of the Hebrew Bible, since the separation of Christianity from Judaism only intensified after AD 135. The process of the formation of the New

Testament canon, i. e. deciding which writings were to be part of the New Testament, only began in the middle of the second century. For the problem of the terms Old Testament/New Testament *see* **Hebrew Bible**.

Pharisee: the Hebrew means 'separated ones'. A Jewish religious group which made the study of the Torah and the scrupulous observance of its regulations the main goal in life. They are mentioned often in the New Testament. After the fall of Jerusalem and the destruction of the temple in AD 70 they were the party which ensured the survival of Judaism, now in 'rabbinic' form.
See Stemberger, *Jewish Contemporaries of Jesus;* Sanders, *Judaism*

Poll tax: In the Roman empire all subjects in the provinces had to pay the so-called poll tax (*tributum capitis*): every male Jew from the age of fourteen and every female Jew from the age of twelve. Only Roman citizens were exempt. Information about the level of the poll tax differs. It was particularly hard on those who had no land and whose only 'resource' was their body or their capacity to work.
See Wengst, *Pax Romana.*

Prophecy: a movement within Judaism essentially before the exile in which individual figures proclaimed God's will for the people. In the first century a number of figures, including Jesus, revived the features of prophecy, usually at the cost of their lives.

See Blenkinsopp, *A History of Prophecy*

Proselytes: people from the nations who joined Jewish communities and adopted the Jewish way of life.

Qumran: a settlement seven or eight miles south of Jericho on the north-west shore of the Dead Sea. From *c.* 180 BC to AD 68 a group lived there which had formed from the Jerusalem priesthood but had distanced itself from both temple and priesthood. The strict observance of rules of cleanness and the understanding of the community as a temple of God are characteristics of the lifestyle of this group. There is no mention of the Qumran community in the New Testament.
See Vermes, *Introduction to the Complete Dead Sea Scrolls*

Rabbis: Jewish scholars who expounded the written and oral Torah in everyday life. They created the Talmud and developed Jewish biblical exegesis further. They paid special attention to religious practice, as is evident from the discussions of the Torah recorded in the Talmud.
See Stemberger, *Jewish Contemporaries of Jesus;* Sanders, *Judaism*

Sabbath: a weekly day of rest and celebration on which all men and women—slaves and foreigners are specifically included—and animals are to recover from work and turn to God. The sabbath begins at dusk on Friday and ends at sunset on Saturday. The observation of the sabbath rest was regarded as a religious confession, particularly in times of foreign rule, expulsion and flight, when the identity of the Jewish people was in danger. The sabbath regulations and their implementation were not uniform, even in the time of Jesus. This is also confirmed by the discussions between Jesus and the Pharisees/scribes, which were about different views of sabbath rest and ultimately about a concrete sabbath *halakhah* adapted to the situation and based on the Torah.
See Sanders, *Judaism*

Sanhedrin: the name for the 'Supreme Council' of the temple of Jerusalem. It was the highest governing body and consisted of the high priest, who came from the Jewish aristocracy, and seventy-one elders. In ancient Judaism the Sanhedrin enjoyed supreme religious, political and legal authority and represented the Jews in Palestine, but it had no influence on Roman policy. Thus for example under Roman rule the Sanhedrin could not impose the death penalty.
See Légasse, *Trial of Jesus*

Shoah/Holocaust: Shoah (annihilation) and Holocaust (whole burnt offering) are two terms for the murder of six million Jews which was systematically carried out by the Nazi regime in Germany (1933–1945). Racist antisemitism, coupled with theological anti-Judaism, served the Hitler regime as the basis for the genocide of the Jewish people. After the Shoah, Christian theology above all has the

responsibility of recognizing the legacy of anti-Jewish theological ideology as such in order to fundamentally redefine the relationships between Jews and Christians. A positive reference to the Jewish roots of the Christian tradition is a step along this way. Here we should note that the Jewish religion must not be commandeered and that Christian identity must be reformulated and confessed without any claim to domination.
See Rubenstein and Roth, *Approaches to Auschwitz*

Sin: understood in Judaism and Christianity as separation from God and God's will, i. e. from life in all its fullness for the whole created order.
See Sanders, *Paul and Palestinian Judaism*

Social history of early Christianity: The analysis of the social context of Judaism and early Christianity is a central element in interpretation of the Bible in terms of social history. The New Testament texts reflect the life lived by the so-called little people in the Roman empire, the poor, the unemployed and the sick, and the life of the oppressed Jewish people as a community. It is from this perspective—from below—that the New Testament takes up political, economic and religious questions which must be investigated historically by exegetes today. Similarly, it is the task of a social history of early Christianity in its exegesis of the texts to take note of the perspective of the New Testament, which is critical of

rulers, so that the 'hymnbook of the poor' is not turned into a theology of rule.

Special material: *see* **Logia source**

Synagogue: The synagogue (from the Greek *synago* = 'gather', 'assemble') can denote both the place where the Jewish community in a town or a village gather and the community itself. The synagogue was the central element of public social and religious life. Here on the sabbath the Torah was read and prayers were offered; during the week it was a school, a lodging for strangers and an information centre. The governing body of a Jewish community was the council of elders, which had limited competence in the sphere of administration and jurisprudence. It was subordinate to the Sanhedrin at the Jerusalem temple.
See Grabbe, *Judaism from Cyrus to Hadrian;* Rousseau and Arav, *Jesus and His World*

Talmud: The Talmud ('study', 'teaching') is the main work of rabbinic Judaism and consists of the Mishnah ('repetition', 'teaching') and the Gemara ('completion', 'what is learned'). The Mishnah, which was revised in the third century, contains religious precepts and regulations relating to civil law, about which there are discussions in the Gemara, which was composed later in the rabbinic schools of Palestine and Babylon. The Palestinian Talmud was completed at the end of the fifth century AD, the Babylonian Talmud at the end of the sixth/beginning of the seventh. The Talmud is

of considerable importance for New Testament scholars since it also discusses traditions which were already in existence in the time of Jesus.
See Musaph-Andriesse, *From Torah to Kabbalah*

Tax collectors: Tax collectors were people who collected tolls and taxes for the Roman government either as contractors or as direct employees. For both categories the pressure to collect enough tax to make a profit was great and it explains the avoidance of taxes, i. e. cheating. Only a few tax collectors must have become rich. Inscriptions indicate that women, too, were involved in this work.
See Wengst, *Pax Romana;* Rousseau and Arav, *Jesus and His World*

Temple: The temple mentioned in the New Testament was built after the end of the Babylonian exile (536–516 BC). It was damaged in 63 BC when Jerusalem was conquered by Pompey. Herod the Great began to renovate it and extend it in 19 BC. The temple was destroyed by the Romans in AD 70, a few years after its completion. It was the religious and national centre of ancient Judaism, a place of worship and thus a holy place. Its centre was the Holy of Holies, which was regarded as the dwelling place of the presence of God. Sacrificial worship was bound up with the temple.
See Sanders, *Judaism;* Rousseau and Arav, *Jesus and His World*

Chronological Table

37–4 BC	Herod rules as a vassal king of Rome, having conquered Jerusalem with the help of Jewish troops.	AD 41–44	Herod Agrippa rules as king.
		AD 41–54	Claudius is emperor.
		AD 44	Agrippa I dies; Judaea becomes a Roman province.
27 BC–AD 14	Augustus is emperor.		
4 BC	Death of Herod; Rome divides his kingdom between his sons Archelaus, Herod Antipas and Philip.	AD 54–68	Nero is emperor.
		AD 66	Beginning of the Jewish revolt against Rome.
		AD 68/69	Destruction of the settlement of Qumran.
AD 6	Archelaus rules as ethnarch of Judaea and Samaria. At this time Jesus is born.	AD 69–79	Vespasian is emperor.
		AD 70	Titus captures and destroys Jerusalem and the temple.
4 BC–AD 39	Herod Antipas rules as tetrarch of Galilee and Peraea.	after AD 70	Rabbinic schools tolerated by Rome take over tasks of the former Sanhedrin; the written versions of the New Testament Gospels come into being.
4 BC–AD 34	Philip rules in northern Transjordan.		
AD 6	Archelaus is deposed; Judaea becomes a procuratorial province and is subject to direct Roman rule; there is a census (numbering of the people) by Quirinius, the governor of Syria.		
		AD 81–96	Domitian is emperor.
		AD 98–117	Trajan is emperor.
		AD 117–138	Hadrian is emperor.
		AD 130	The emperor Hadrian decides to transform Jerusalem into the eastern imperial metropolis of Aelia Capitolina.
AD 6–15	Annas is high priest.		
AD 14–37	Tiberius is emperor.		
AD 18–36	Caiaphas is high priest.	AD 132–135	Bar Kochba revolt.
AD 26–36	Pontius Pilate is governor of Judaea. At this time Jesus was crucified. The oral traditions about Jesus come into being after his death.	AD 135	Jerusalem renamed Aelia Capitolina; complete expulsion of the Jewish population from Jerusalem; the separation of the followers of Jesus Christ from Judaism intensifies.
AD 37–41	Caligula is emperor.		

Bibliography

The books mentioned here represent a selection which report on scholarly discussions and results in a way which lay people can understand.

Blenkinsopp, Joseph, *A History of Prophecy in Israel*, Westminster John Knox Press 1998
An up-to-date text book.

Countryman, L. William, *Dirt, Greed and Sex*, Fortress Press and SCM Press 1988
Shows how different biblical ideas are from our own in areas of purity and property.

Crüsemann, Frank, *The Torah. Theology and Social History of Old Testament Law*, T & T Clark 1996
A thorough but highly readable account of the history and exegesis of the legal texts of the Torah. The author shows the social-historical context of the Torah and opens up a new perspective on its differentiated ethics. A book which is indispensable for New Testament exegesis.

Farmer, William R. (ed), *Anti-Judaism and the Gospels*, Trinity Press International 1999
A collection of essays by experts investigating how far hostility to Judaism can be found in the Gospels and the motives behind it.

Grabbe, Lester L., *Judaism from Cyrus to Hadrian*, Fortress Press 1992 and SCM Press 1994

A reliable and accurate account of the sources, the problems and the range of scholarly opinions relating to Judaism in the time of Jesus, before and after.

Josephus, Flavius, *The Jewish War*, translated by G. A. Williamson, Penguin Books 1959
The most important contemporary source for life in Palestine in the first Christian century.

Kuschel, Karl-Josef, *The Poet as Mirror*, SCM Press 1999
God, Jesus and human nature as reflected in twentieth-century literature.

Légasse, Simon, *The Trial of Jesus*, SCM Press 1997
A thorough discussion of all the issues relating to the different accounts of the trial of Jesus in the Gospels.

Musaph-Andriesse, R. C., *From Torah to Kabbalah. A Basic Introduction to the Writings of Judaism*, SCM Press 1981
A handy guide to all the Jewish writings referred to in this book.

Plaskow, Judith, *Standing again at Sinai. Judaism from a Feminist Perspective*, Harper and Row 1990
A Jewish writer reflects on the problems posed to women by the male-dominated Jewish tradition.

Rousseau, John J. and **Arav, Rami**, *Jesus and His World. An Archaeological and Cultural Dictionary*, SCM Press and Fortress Press 1996
A survey with photographs, line drawings and maps, of every

aspect of the world in which Jesus lived, by a Christian scholar and a Jewish one.

Rowland, Christopher, *Christian Origins. An Account of the Setting and Character of the most Important Messianic Sect of Judaism,* SPCK 1985
An important and readable text-book setting Christianity firmly in its Jewish background.

Rubenstein, Richard L. and **Roth, John K.,** *Approches to Auschwitz: The Legacy of the Holocaust,* John Knox Press and SCM Press 1987
Traces antisemitism throughout history, events leading to the Holocaust, its implementation and responses to it. No other single work contains such a wide range of material on the Holocaust.

Sanders, E. P., *Jesus and Judaism,* SCM Press and Fortress Press 1985
Recognized as one of the best books about Jesus to have been written in the twentieth century, firmly rooting Jesus in his contemporary setting.

Sanders, E. P., *Judaism. Practice and Belief, 63 BCE–66 CE,* SCM Press and Trinity Press International 1992
Probably the definitive work on Judaism in the time of Jesus.

Sanders, E. P., *Paul and Palestinian Judaism,* SCM Press and Fortress Press 1977
Shows that Judaism in Palestine at the time of Jesus and Paul was a much more joyful and positive religion than it is usually made out to be.

Schottroff, Luise, *Lydia's Impatient Sisters. A Feminist Social History of Early Christianity,* Westminster John Knox Press and SCM Press 1995

The social history which has been mentioned in this biography can be checked with information from sources outside the New Testament (non-literary sources from the spheres of Judaism, Hellenism and the Roman Empire). An evaluation of this source material and the reasons for the decisions about the method adopted by the present book (dealing with the 'historical' Jesus, theories about the parables) are given here.

Schottroff, Luise, and **Wacker, Marie-Theres** (eds), *Feminist Interpretation: The Bible in Women's Perspective,* Fortress Press 1998
Survey information about the international feminist exegetical discussion, also on the Gospels, which are the main sources of information about the historical Jesus.

Schüssler Fiorenza, Elisabeth, *In Memory of Her. A Feminist Theo-logical Reconstruction of Christian Origins,* Crossroad Publishing Company and SCM Press ²1994
An alternative light on the beginnings of Christianity from a woman's perspective, bringing out the varied national, cultural, social and religious backgrounds of Christianity

Soelle, Dorothee, *Thinking about God. An Introduction to Theology,* SCM Press and Trinity Press International 1998
Explains for non-theologians the main themes of Christian faith like the Bible, creation, sin and grace on the basis of three schemes: orthodox theology, liberal theology and liberation theology.

Stemberger, Gunter, *Jewish Contemp-oraries of Jesus. Pharisees, Saddu-cees, Essenes,* Fortress Press 1995

A good basic introduction to the main currents of Judaism at the time of Jesus.

Theissen, Gerd, and **Merz, Annette**, *The Historical Jesus. A Comprehensive Guide*, SCM Press and Fortress Press 1998
A scholarly survey of all the relevant issues in research into Jesus, above all from the nineteenth century to the present. This text book can easily be read by non-specialists.

Vermes, Geza, *An Introduction to the Complete Dead Sea Scrolls*, SCM Press and Fortress Press 1999
A description of all the Dead Sea Scrolls with an account of the nature of the Qumran sect and its beliefs.

Vermes, Geza, *Jesus the Jew. A Historian Reads the Gospels*, SCM Press and Fortress Press 1973
An account of Jesus by a historian with a Jewish perspective.

Wengst, Klaus, *Pax Romana and the Peace of Jesus Christ*, SCM Press 1987
By means of numerous contemporary sources the author portrays the social and economic structures of the Roman empire and the situation of the Jesus movement.

Index of Biblical References

Index of Names

Sources of the Poems

p. 11 Bertolt Brecht, *Gesammelte Werke, Gedichte II*, © Suhrkamp Verlag, Frankfurt am Main 1967, p. 104.

p. 12 Dorothee Soelle, *Meditationen und Gebrauchstexte*, © Fietkau Verlag Berlin 1974, p.14.

p. 15 Dorothee Soelle, *Die revolutionäre Geduld*, © Fietkau Verlag Berlin 1969, p. 29.

p. 20 Wolf Biermann, *Lieder vom Preussischen Ikarus*, © Verlag Kiepenheuer und Witsch, Cologne 1978.

p. 30 Dorothee Soelle.

pp. 32f. Kurt Marti, *Abendland. Gedichte*, © Radius Verlag, Stuttgart 1980, pp. 45f.

pp. 54f. Dorothee Soelle, *Fliegen lernen. Gedichte*, © Fietkau Verlag Berlin 1979, p. 9.

pp. 66f. Rudolf Otto Wiemer, *Ernstfall. Gedichte*, © Steinkopf Verlag Kiel, Stuttgart 1973, pp. 75f.

p. 68 Dorothee Soelle, *Die revolutionäre Geduld*, © Fietkau Verlag Berlin 1969, p. 13.

p. 70 Nelly Sachs, *Fahrt ins Staublose*, © Suhrkamp Verlag Frankfurt am Main 1961, pp. 92–94.

p. 73 Harold A. Carter, *The Prayer Tradition of Black People*, Judson Press, Valley Forge 1976, pp. 49–51.

pp. 76f. Vilma Sturm in Dorothee Soelle and Fulbert Stefensky, *Politisches Nachgebet in Köln*, Stuttgart and Mainz 1969, pp. 107f.

pp. 86f. Antonio Reiser and Paul Gerhard Schoenborn in id.

(eds), *Sehnsucht nach dem Fest der freien Menschen. Gebete aus Lateinamerika*, Wuppertal and Gelnhausen 1982, p. 53.

p. 89 Ernesto Cardenal, from *Oración por Marilyn Monroe (Prayer for Marilyn Monroe)*.

p. 94 A song from Brazil, author unknown, in Prelazio do Xingu (ed), *Acorda América*, Altamira 1993, p. 127.

pp. 106f. Else Lasker-Schüler, *Gedichte*, © Suhrkamp Verlag, Frankfurt am Main 1996.

pp. 110f. Dorothee Soelle.

p. 111 Carola Moosbach, *Gottflamme Du Schöne. Lob- und Klagegebete*, © Gütersloher Verlagshaus 1997, p. 24.

p. 121 Rudolf Otto Wiemer, *Ernstfall. Gedichte*, © Steinkopf Verlag, Kiel and Stuttgart 1973, p. 300.

p. 122 Erich Kästner, *Gesammelte Schriften, Band 1, Gedichte*, © Erich Kästner Archiv, RA Beisler, Munich 1959, p. 141.

pp. 126f. Luise Schottroff, 'Sündenbekenntnis' in Dorothee Soelle and Luise Schottroff, *Die Erde gehört Gott. Ein Kapitel feministischer Befreiungstheologie*, © Peter Hammer Verlag, Wuppertal 1995, pp.54f.

p. 128 Dorothee Soelle.

pp. 136f. Dorothee Soelle, *Meditationen und Gebrauchstexte*, © Fietkau Verlag Berlin 1974, p. 10.

p. 138 Dorothee Soelle, *Fliegen lernen. Gedichte*, © Fietkau Verlag Berlin 1979, p. 21.

Sources of the Illustrations

Archiv für Kunst und Geschichte, Berlin   24, 26, 52

Archivi Alinari, Florence   12, 31, 60

Bednorz, Achim, Cologne   65

British Museum, London   34, 46

British Royal Family   19

Cuenca, Sammlung Bertha Cisneros de Cueva, Ecuador   18

Delaware Art Museum, Samuel and Mary R. Bancroft Memorial Collection   21

Diözesanmuseum, Freising   7

Duby Tal/Albatross   57

Giraudon, Paris   29

Herder Verlag, Freiburg   3

India Office Library, London (E. T. Archive)   39

Metropolitan Museum of Art, New York , Rogers Fund, 1956   56

Ministero Beni Culturali e Ambientali   43

Monika Nikolic, Kassel   4

Musée d'Orsay, Paris   61, 70

Musée du Louvre, Paris   9, 53

Musée National des Thermes et de l'Hotel de Cluny, Paris   35

Museo del Prado, Madrid   72

Museo Nazionale, Naples   20

Museum Unterlinden, Colmar   16, 40

National Gallery, London   10, 37

Ono-Feller, Masami, Bergisch Gladbach   68

Pinacoteca Nazionale, Bologna   67

Fonteficia Commissione di Archeologia Sacra, Rome   32, 33

Rheims, Bettina   64

Rheinisches Landesmuseum, Bonn   47

Rheinisches Landesmuseum, Trier   44

Scala, Florence   25, 27

Scala/ArtResource, N.Y.   49

Schmitz, Heinz, Cologne   2, 24

Shai Ginott, Tel Aviv   15

Sonia Halliday and Laura Lushington   14

Hermitage Museum, St Petersburg   71

Ethnographic Museum, St Petersburg   38

Stiftsbibliothek St Peter, Salzburg   55

The Brooklyn Museum/John Neitzel   36

The Walters Art Museum, Baltimore   1

Uni Dia Verlag, Munich   45

Vatican, Museo Missionario Etnologico   74